Lantana CAFE
BREAKFAST & BRUNCH

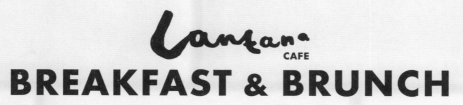

Lantana CAFE
BREAKFAST & BRUNCH

Relaxed recipes to start each day

SHELAGH RYAN

with photography by
KATE WHITAKER & ADRIAN LAWRENCE

RYLAND PETERS & SMALL
LONDON • NEW YORK

Senior Designers Toni Kay and Megan Smith
Editors Miriam Catley and Stephanie Milner
Head of Production Patricia Harrington
Art Director Leslie Harrington
Editorial Director Julia Charles
Publisher Cindy Richards

Prop Stylist Tony Hutchinson
Food Stylists Lucy McElvie and Sarah Cook
Assistant Food Stylist Ellie Jarvis
Indexer Vanessa Bird

First published in 2018 by
Ryland Peters & Small
20–21 Jockey's Fields,
London WC1R 4BW
and
341 E 116th St, New York NY 10029
www.rylandpeters.com

Text © Shelagh Ryan 2014, 2018
Design and photographs ©
Ryland Peters & Small 2014, 2018

A selection of the recipes in this book were
originally published by Ryland Peters & Small
in 2015 in *Café Kitchen*

ISBN: 978-1-84975-972-4

Printed and bound in China

10 9 8 7 6 5 4 3 2 1

A CIP record for this book is available from the British Library.

US Library of Congress Cataloging-in-Publication Data has been
applied for.

NOTES
• Both British (Metric) and American (Imperial plus US cups)
measurements and ingredients are included in these recipes for
your convenience, however it is important to work with one set of
measurements and not alternate between the two within a recipe.
Spellings are primarily British.
• All spoon measurements are level unless otherwise specified.
• All eggs are medium (UK) or large (US), unless specified as large,
in which case US extra-large should be used. Uncooked or partially
cooked eggs should not be served to the very old, frail, young
children, pregnant women or those with compromised immune
systems.
• When a recipe calls for the grated zest of citrus fruit, buy unwaxed
fruit and wash well before using. If you can only find treated fruit,
scrub well in warm, soapy water before using.
• Ovens should be preheated to the specified temperatures. We
recommend using an oven thermometer. If using a fan-assisted oven,
adjust temperatures according to the manufacturer's instructions.
• Sterilize preserving jars before use. Wash them in hot, soapy water
and rinse in boiling water. Place in a large saucepan and then cover
with hot water. With the lid on, bring the water to the boil and
continue boiling for 15 minutes. Turn off the heat, then leave the
jars in the hot water until just before they are to be filled. Invert the
jars onto clean paper towels to dry. Sterilize the lids for 5 minutes,
by boiling, or according to the manufacturer's instructions. Jars
should be filled and sealed while they are still hot.

All photography by Kate Whitaker apart from:

Jan Baldwin page 91

Peter Cassidy page 101

Adrian Lawrence pages 2–3, 7, 15, 18–19, 22,
31al, 33–37, 42, 44, 52, 55, 64, 78, 81bl, 93, 96,
100, 104, 131, 135, 136, endpapers insert

William Reavell page 14

CONTENTS

INTRODUCTION

We wouldn't dream of eating the same meal for dinner day after day but at breakfast time many of us fall into a monotonous routine of toast and cereal. Respect for the first meal of the day was part of my upbringing. During the week my mum would diligently squeeze us orange juice every morning and regularly served a cooked breakfast before sending us off to school. On the weekend the kitchen was my father's domain and he loved nothing more than a leisurely Sunday brunch on the veranda, reading the newspapers (this was Queensland, not London). These brunches were the inspiration for many of the dishes on Lantana's menu, including Baked Eggs with Chorizo (page 27), Banana Pancakes (page 35) and Bubble and Squeak (page 39) which dad would make with the leftover vegetables from our Saturday night roast dinner.

I'm one of those annoying morning people that wake early and full of energy. I know that many people are barely conscious when they roll out of bed and find it hard to be too adventurous with breakfast, especially if you need to be out the door in 10 minutes. But for those days when you have the luxury of time, breakfast, or brunch as it drifts closer to lunchtime, can be gloriously indulgent whether preparing it just for yourself, your family, or for friends as a more relaxed way to entertain. A pan of Slow Braised Beans with Ham Hock (page 50), some Cheddar Cornbread (page 102) and a Bloody Mary (page 138) is a great way to feed, and impress, a crowd.

I love it when customers in our cafés ask for a recipe or I overhear a table discussing their meal, trying to put their finger on a particular ingredient so they can recreate the dish themselves. Imitation is the sincerest form of flattery and many of the recipes in this book are ones that Lantana customers enjoy and have repeatedly requested. Now celebrating our tenth year, it seems the perfect opportunity to share the recipes that have stood the test of time.

Adaptability is an essential part of the way I think about food and recipes. I encourage you to be creative with the recipes and mix and match them at will. The Sriracha Hollandaise (page 43) is delicious with Smoked Haddock Fishcakes (page 24), Pulled Pork (page 32) makes a fine hash instead of duck (page 36) and Chilli Jam (page 124) makes pretty much everything taste better. When I have time at the weekend I like to make batches of things that can be stored (such as the Toasted Muesli on page 10), refrigerated (Poached Fruit page 17) or frozen (Courgette Bread on page 98) and enjoyed throughout the week.

Start your day as you mean to go on and savour every mouthful. I hope these recipes will provide you with endless variety and inspiration. You might just find yourself becoming an annoying morning person.

FRUIT, OATS & GRAINS

TOASTED MUESLI WITH BAKED RHUBARB

Making muesli is one of the comforting rituals in my life. I love filling my shopping bag with oats, nuts, seeds and dried fruit, mixing all the ingredients together and slowly toasting them in the oven.

100 ml/⅓ cup sunflower oil
½ teaspoon pure vanilla extract
125 ml/½ cup clear honey
125 ml/½ cup maple syrup
¼ teaspoon ground cinnamon
500 g/2½ cups jumbo rolled oats
150 g/1½ cups rolled barley flakes
70 g/⅔ cup wheatgerm
50 g/⅔ cup dried desiccated/
    shredded coconut
125 g/1¼ cups almonds
100 g/1 cup pecans
125 g/scant 1 cup sunflower seeds
100 g/⅔ cup pumpkin seeds
10 g/1 tablespoon sesame seeds
250 g/1⅔ cups (dark) raisins
200 g/1½ cups dried pitted dates,
    halved
Greek yogurt, to serve

BAKED RHUBARB
500 g/5 cups rhubarb, trimmed
    and cut into 5-cm/2-inch pieces
2 tablespoons caster/granulated
    sugar
grated zest and freshly squeezed
    juice of 1 orange

*2 baking sheets, greased and
    lined with baking parchment*

SERVES 10

Preheat the oven to 120°C (250°F) Gas ½.

Pour the oil, vanilla, honey, syrup and cinnamon into a saucepan set over a gentle heat and stir to combine.

Mix together all the remaining ingredients, except the (dark) raisins, dates and yogurt in a large mixing bowl. Pour over the hot oil mixture and stir well to ensure everything is well coated.

Spread the mixture onto the prepared baking sheets and bake in the preheated oven for 30–45 minutes. Stir the mixture at regular intervals and cook until evenly golden and dry. Remove from the oven and set aside to cool completely before adding the (dark) raisins and dates.

To make the Baked Rhubarb, preheat the oven to 150°C (300°F) Gas 2. Place the rhubarb in a baking pan that is big enough to hold it in a single layer. Sprinkle over the sugar and orange zest and juice, and gently mix together. Cover with foil and bake in the preheated oven for 30–45 minutes, until the rhubarb is just soft. Remove from the oven and set aside to cool completely before serving with the toasted muesli and Greek yogurt.

Store any leftover muesli and baked rhubarb in separate airtight containers. The muesli will keep at room temperature for up to 2 weeks, and the rhubarb should be kept in the fridge for 3–5 days.

BIRCHER MUESLI WITH FRESH BERRIES

A fantastic alternative to porridge for summer, this is one of those recipes that can be modified ad infinitum. Try substituting the apple juice with orange or cranberry, add pumpkin seeds, macadamia nuts, dried apricots or any dried or poached fruit.

250 g/1 1/4 cups jumbo rolled oats
30 g/1/3 cup (dark) raisins
375 ml/1 1/2 cups apple juice
30 g/1/3 cup whole almonds
grated zest and freshly squeezed
  juice of 1/2 lemon
1 apple or pear, coarsely grated
125 ml/1/2 cup natural/plain
  yogurt

TO SERVE
mixed fresh berries
clear honey

a baking sheet, greased and
  lined with baking parchment

SERVES 4

Place the oats and raisins in a large mixing bowl and pour over the apple juice. Cover with clingfilm/plastic wrap and chill in the fridge for at least an hour, preferably overnight.

Preheat the oven to 180°C (350°F) Gas 4.

Scatter the almonds onto the prepared baking sheet and toast in the preheated oven for about 10 minutes.

Remove from the oven and set aside to cool before chopping to a rough texture. Remove the soaked oat mixture from the fridge. Uncover and add the lemon zest and juice, chopped toasted almonds and grated apple or pear. Stir to combine.

Add the yogurt, a little at a time, stirring after each addition to your desired consistency. Serve in bowls with fresh berries on top and a drizzle of honey.

STRAWBERRY, BANANA & ALMOND SMOOTHIE BOWL

This is definitely a dish for the Instagrammers as it looks so pretty with all of its colourful adornments. Feel free to substitute different fruits, nut butters and toppings that you have to hand. To make this a fast and easy weekday breakfast, freeze small bags with the banana, strawberries and oats ready to whizz up with the milk, yogurt and nut butter before adding your toppings.

200 g/1 cup strawberries, frozen
1 banana, peeled and frozen
60 g/generous ½ cup jumbo
rolled oats
125 ml/½ cup almond milk
120 g/½ cup Greek yogurt
(or coconut yogurt for a
vegan version)
30 g/2 tablespoons almond butter
(or any nut butter)
10 g/2 teaspoons clear honey
(or maple syrup for a
vegan version)

TO SERVE
blueberries, sliced banana,
toasted muesli, goji berries
and/or chia seeds

SERVES 1

Place all the smoothie ingredients into a blender and blitz until smooth.

Pour into a shallow bowl and decorate with blueberries, sliced banana, toasted muesli, goji berries and/or chia seeds. Serve.

VERJUICE POACHED FRUIT

The magic ingredient in our poached fruit is verjuice, a juice made from unfermented grapes, but if you can't find this, use a combination of apple and lemon juice or a dry wine.

500 ml/2 cups verjuice (or 500 ml/2 cups apple juice mixed with the freshly squeezed juice of 1 lemon)

½ vanilla pod/bean, sliced lengthways

a pinch of saffron strands

1 cinnamon stick

250 g/1¼ cups caster/granulated sugar

freshly squeezed juice of ½ orange, plus the skin

750 g/3 cups (about 5 medium) peeled, cored and quartered pears

300 g/3 cups (about 2 medium) peeled, cored and quartered green apples

100 g/scant ⅔ cup (about 4) pitted and quartered plums

250 g/2½ cups rhubarb, trimmed and cut into 4-cm/1½-inch pieces

TO SERVE
150 g/1½ cups blueberries
Greek yogurt

SERVES 6

Pour 750 ml/3 cups of water with the verjuice (or substitute) into a heavy-bottomed saucepan or pot set over a medium-high heat. Add the vanilla pod/bean, including the seeds scraped out with the back of a sharp knife, the saffron, cinnamon and sugar. Squeeze the juice from the orange half into the pan and put the squeezed skin in too. Bring the liquid to the boil, then reduce the heat and simmer for 15 minutes.

Add the quartered pears to the simmering poaching liquor, cover the surface with a circle of baking parchment to keep the fruit submerged and cook for about 15 minutes. The pears should be tender and still hold their shape. Remove the fruit from the pan and transfer to a large mixing bowl. Repeat with the other fruits, poaching each separately for the following times: the apples for 8–10 minutes, the plums for 5 minutes and the rhubarb for 3 minutes.

When all the fruit is cooked, increase the heat and simmer the liquor for a further 5 minutes to reduce it to a syrup. Remove the pan from the heat and let the syrup cool completely before pouring it over the poached fruit. Remove and discard the cinnamon stick, vanilla pod/bean and orange skin, if you like.

Add the blueberries just before serving and serve the fruit in bowls with some syrup drizzled over and a dollop of Greek yogurt.

COCONUT CHIA PUDDING POTS WITH COCONUT YOGURT, MANGO, GINGER, MINT & POMEGRANATE SEEDS

These little pots are deceptively decadent and delicious despite containing no dairy or refined sugar. They're a lighter and healthier alternative to your traditional oat-based breakfasts.

1 ripe mango, peeled, pitted and finely diced
2 teaspoons ginger syrup
freshly chopped leaves from 4 sprigs of mint
coconut yogurt, to serve
seeds from ½ pomegranate, to serve

CHIA PUDDING MIX
400 ml/1²/₃ cups coconut milk
1 tablespoon clear honey
4 cardamom pods, lightly bruised
1 teaspoon pure vanilla extract
165 g/1 cup chia seeds

SERVES 4

To make the chia pudding mix, put the coconut milk, honey, cardamom pods and vanilla into a saucepan and heat until it just reaches the boil. Remove from the heat and leave to infuse for at least 20 minutes, or until cool.

Strain the mix into a large bowl and discard the cardamom pods. Stir in the chia seeds and whisk for 1–2 minutes making sure the chia seeds don't clump together. Cover with clingfilm/plastic wrap and leave overnight or for a minimum of 4 hours in the fridge. The chia seeds will swell so make sure your bowl has plenty of room.

Put the mango flesh into a bowl with the ginger syrup. Add the chopped mint and gently combine.

Spoon the chia pudding mix into four serving glasses and top each with a dollop of coconut yogurt, the mango and mint, and a sprinkling of pomegranate seeds. Serve.

FRENCH TOAST WITH HONEY ROAST FIGS, ORANGE MASCARPONE & TOASTED ALMONDS

Nothing says 'Saturday morning' better than French toast. The orange mascarpone cuts perfectly through the thick, eggy brioche.

125 ml/½ cup mascarpone
2 tablespoons single/light cream
½ teaspoon grated orange zest, plus extra to serve
1 tablespoon freshly squeezed orange juice
4 ripe figs, cut in half lengthways
clear honey, to drizzle
100 g/3½ oz. whole almonds
2 eggs
100 ml/⅓ cup milk
¼ teaspoon pure vanilla extract
1 tablespoon caster/granulated sugar
2–4 thick slices of brioche
unsalted butter, for frying
icing/confectioners' sugar, for dusting

2 baking sheets, greased and lined with baking parchment

SERVES 2

Preheat the oven to 180°C (350°F) Gas 4.

Mix the mascarpone with the cream, orange zest and juice in a small mixing bowl. Cover and set aside.

Place the figs, cut-side up, on a prepared baking sheet. Drizzle with honey and roast in the preheated oven for 15–20 minutes until soft and caramelized. Remove from the oven and set aside. Meanwhile, scatter the almonds on the other prepared baking sheet and bake in the oven for 8–10 minutes until lightly golden. Remove from the oven, cool completely, then roughly chop if desired.

To make the French toast, whisk together the eggs with the milk in a large mixing bowl. Add the vanilla and caster/granulated sugar, and whisk again. Transfer to a shallow dish and set aside.

Melt a little butter in a large frying pan/skillet set over a medium heat. Dip each slice of brioche in the egg mixture one at a time. Let the slices soak up the mixture for a few seconds, then turn over to coat the other side.

Place the egg-soaked brioche in the hot pan, one slice at a time, and cook until golden on the bottom. Turn over and cook for a few minutes longer until both sides are golden. Transfer to a clean baking sheet and put in the oven to keep warm. Cook the remaining slices in the same way, adding a little more butter to the pan, if required. To serve, cut the brioche slices in half, overlap the slices on the plate and top with the figs, mascarpone and almonds. Sprinkle with a little orange zest and icing/confectioners' sugar, and serve.

EGGS

SMOKED HADDOCK FISHCAKES
WITH POACHED EGGS & DILL MAYO

The subtle saltiness of smoked fish provides a lovely contrast
to the creamy yolk of a poached egg.

**700 g/1½ lbs. (about 4 large)
Maris Piper, King Edward or
other floury potatoes**
300 ml/1¼ cups milk
1 bay leaf
**400 g/14 oz. undyed smoked
haddock fillets (skin on)**
25 g/½ cup chives, finely chopped
**20 g/scant ½ cup dill, finely
chopped**
25 g/2 tablespoons melted butter
**1 egg, lightly beaten, plus 6 eggs
for poaching**
**sea salt and freshly ground
black pepper**
vegetable oil, for frying

DILL MAYO
200 ml/¾ cup mayonnaise
1 tablespoon freshly chopped dill
**½ teaspoon freshly grated
lemon zest**
**1 tablespoon freshly squeezed
lemon juice**

TO SERVE
a bunch of fresh watercress
2 tablespoons olive oil
freshly squeezed juice of 1 lemon

*a baking sheet lined with
clingfilm/plastic wrap*

**MAKES 12 CAKES
FOR 6 PEOPLE**

Put the whole potatoes with their skin on in a large pot filled with water set over a medium-high heat. Boil for 15–20 minutes, or until cooked through. Drain and transfer to a plate to cool. Cover and chill in the fridge for at least 2 hours, or preferably overnight.

To prepare the haddock, place the milk and bay leaf in a large frying pan/skillet set over a medium heat and bring to the boil. Add the haddock, skin-side down. Reduce the heat and simmer for 3 minutes. Flip the fillets over, turn off the heat and allow the haddock to continue to cook in the residual heat.

Peel and grate the potatoes into a large bowl and discard the skin. Add the chopped herbs, melted butter, beaten egg, salt and pepper and mix well. Lift the haddock out of the milk, remove the skin and discard along with the milk and bay leaf. Flake the fish into chunks and add to the potato mix. Stir to combine, taking care not to break up the fish too much. Form 12 round patties with your hands, of about 90 g/3¼ oz. each. Place the fishcakes on the prepared baking sheet, cover with clingfilm/plastic wrap and place in the fridge for at least 1 hour.

When ready to serve, preheat the oven to 160°C (325°F) Gas 3. Heat 2 tablespoons of oil in a non-stick frying pan/skillet. Fry the fishcakes in batches for 3–4 minutes each side until lightly golden. Transfer to a baking sheet and keep warm in the oven while you cook the remaining fishcakes, adding more oil to the pan each time.

To poach the eggs, put a large saucepan of water with a pinch of salt over a medium heat and maintain the water at a gentle simmer. Crack an egg into a cup or ramekin and gently tip it into the pan. Repeat with the other eggs and cook for 4 minutes. Drain on a clean kitchen cloth or paper towels.

Mix all of the ingredients for the Dill Mayo together and season to taste. Serve the fishcakes with a poached egg on top, the Dill Mayo and some watercress dressed with the olive oil and lemon juice.

BAKED EGGS WITH CHORIZO, MUSHROOMS & LEMON CRÈME FRAÎCHE

4 eggs
sea salt and freshly ground
    black pepper
Turkish bread, to serve

CHORIZO SAUCE
1 tablespoon olive oil
1 small red onion, finely chopped
2 garlic cloves, finely sliced
120 g/1 cup chorizo sausages,
    cut into 5-mm/¼-inch slices
1 x 400-g/14-oz. can plum
    tomatoes
1 tablespoon balsamic vinegar
1½ teaspoons soft brown sugar
¼ teaspoon dried chilli/hot red
    pepper flakes
½ star anise
1 x 5-cm/2-inch strip orange rind,
    pith removed
12 basil leaves, roughly torn

BAKED MUSHROOMS
15 g/1 tablespoon butter
1 tablespoon olive oil
1 garlic clove, finely sliced
4 Portobello mushrooms, sliced

LEMON CRÈME FRAÎCHE
100 g/½ cup crème fraîche or
    sour/soured cream
¼ teaspoon grated lemon zest
½ teaspoon freshly squeezed
    lemon juice

a baking sheet, greased

SERVES 4

There are many versions of this Middle Eastern dish on breakfast menus in cafés throughout Australia. I like plenty of sauce, which helps to cook the eggs.

Begin by preparing the Chorizo Sauce. Put the oil in a large heavy-bottomed frying pan/skillet set over a low-medium heat and gently sauté the chopped onion for 7–10 minutes until soft and translucent, but not coloured. Add the sliced garlic and chorizo, and cook until the chorizo starts to brown and release its oils. Add 60 ml/¼ cup of water and all the remaining ingredients except the basil. Season with salt and pepper, turn up the heat and bring the mixture to the boil. Immediately reduce the heat and simmer for 20–30 minutes, until the sauce is thick and glossy. Remove from the heat, discard the star anise and orange rind, stir in the basil and set aside.

Preheat the oven to 180°C (350°F) Gas 4.

To prepare the mushrooms, melt the butter and olive oil in a frying pan/skillet set over a medium heat. Add the sliced garlic and allow it to cook gently for 2–3 minutes, then remove the pan from the heat. Place the mushrooms on the prepared baking sheet and spoon over the garlic-infused butter. Cover with foil and bake in the preheated oven for 15–20 minutes until tender.

To make the Lemon Crème Fraîche, combine all of the ingredients in a small mixing bowl, cover and set aside.

Return the Chorizo Sauce to a low heat and gently reheat. Add the Baked Mushrooms to the pan, making sure they are evenly distributed and half submerged in the sauce. Make four holes in the sauce with a wooden spoon and crack in the eggs. Cover and cook very gently for 15–20 minutes until the whites are set and the yolks still a little runny. Sprinkle with black pepper and serve with Turkish bread and the Lemon Crème Fraîche.

DUKKAH WITH HARD-BOILED EGGS

Dukkah is an Egyptian dry spice blend that has a multitude of uses – as a salad sprinkle, a seasoning, or a dip with bread and olive oil. We serve it as a snack with hard-boiled eggs.

100 g/1 cup whole hazelnuts
20 g/¼ cup pistachio nuts
2 tablespoons coriander seeds
1 tablespoon cumin seeds
5 tablespoons sesame seeds
2 teaspoons white or black peppercorns
½ teaspoon dried chilli/hot red pepper flakes
½ teaspoon sea salt
8 eggs, to serve

MAKES 180 G/1½ CUPS AND SERVES 4

Preheat the oven to 160°C (325°F) Gas 3.

Place the hazelnuts and pistachio nuts on separate small baking sheets and roast in the preheated oven for 10 minutes. Remove from the oven and immediately wrap the hazelnuts in a clean kitchen towel. Set aside to allow the steam to build for a minute before rubbing them within the kitchen towel to remove the loose skins. When both the pistachio nuts and hazelnuts are cool, roughly crush them using a pestle and mortar to a chunky texture. Transfer the mixture to a large mixing bowl.

Place the coriander and cumin seeds in a preheated dry frying pan/skillet set over a medium heat. Dry-fry the seeds for a couple of minutes, shaking the pan from time to time, until they start to pop. Remove the seeds from the pan and crush using a pestle and mortar. Add to the nuts in the mixing bowl.

Place the sesame seeds in the same, dry pan and toast until lightly golden, giving the pan a shake every 30 seconds. Remove from the pan and grind using the pestle and mortar. Add to the nut and seed mixture. Repeat this process with the peppercorns.

Lightly grind the chilli/hot red pepper flakes using the pestle and mortar and add to the nut and seed mixture. Finally, add the salt and mix everything together. The dukkah is now ready and can be stored in an airtight container for up to 2 weeks.

Place the eggs in a saucepan or pot with enough cold water to cover them by 2.5 cm/1 inch. Set over a medium-high heat and bring the water to the boil. As soon as it reaches the boil, reduce the heat and simmer for 7 minutes. Remove the pan from the heat, discard the cooking water and rinse under cold, running water for 1 minute. Set aside to cool completely in the pan filled with cold water. This cooling method helps to prevent a dark ring forming between the yolk and the white. Peel the eggs and dip the tops in the dukkah. They're delicious!

BEST BRUNCH EVER

'Brunch is cheerful, sociable and inciting. It is talk-compelling. It puts you in a good temper, it makes you satisfied with yourself and your fellow beings, it sweeps away the worries and cobwebs of the week.'
GUY BERINGER, 'BRUNCH: A PLEA', 1895.

I came to London on an ambitious mission: to convince the British that there are better ways to start the day than their most significant export, 'The Full English'. Even though our mothers told us that the first meal of the day is the most important, it is the meal that has historically been treated with the least respect, particularly in England. When in a fragile state, it might be a fry-up involving canned beans and fried eggs. When in a hurry, it's a bowl of cold, packet cereal or a processed muffin eaten with a milky, burnt coffee from a coffee chain store on the way to work. Worst of all, it gets missed altogether. As our first meal, it sets the tone for the rest of the day and should be given the care and attention it deserves.

Australia has developed a breakfast and brunch culture which rivals that of New York. It is an extremely social affair and the food is determinably inventive and multicultural. During the week, and always on the weekend, cafés are full of groups of friends sitting down to dishes as varied as miso porridge, a scrambled egg burrito, French toast with labne and orange blossom syrup, or toasted pide with avocado.

Our Lantana cafés in London are open all day, but it is brunch that is our busiest and most popular service. Even though my aim was to convert the Brits to brunch culture, it still surprises me to see people queuing for a table at any café at 9 am. The most unassuming cafés, tucked down a side street, can quickly become places with queues around the block when tweeters and bloggers start spreading the word. Less surprising is the fact that it's the 20- and 30-somethings who have really answered the call to brunch. A lazy Sunday morning with friends is the perfect way to dissect the gossip from the night before, nurse sore heads with a 'hair of the dog' Bloody Mary, and refill empty stomachs with plates of comforting sweet and savoury food.

The growing popularity of brunch also reflects the fact that cafés and restaurants now take this meal seriously. Gone are the days when you'd go out for breakfast and the extent of your choices would be eggs; scrambled, poached or fried. It's not uncommon to find cafés going the extra mile to make their own slow-braised baked beans or smoke their own salmon. And they're rewarded for their efforts when appreciative customers photograph their meal to share with the world. #bestbruncheyer

SLOW PULLED PORK DROWNED EGGS

1 boneless shoulder of pork, skin on (approx. 2–2.5 kg/4½–5½ lbs.)
vegetable oil, for frying

MARINADE
200 ml/¾ cup tomato ketchup
30 ml/2 tablespoons soy sauce
3 garlic cloves, minced
1 tablespoon smoked paprika
1 teaspoon dried chilli/hot red pepper flakes
200 g/1 cup soft dark brown sugar
1 tablespoon celery salt
70 ml/scant ⅓ cup cider vinegar

TOMATO SAUCE
2 tablespoons olive oil
2 onions, diced
2 garlic cloves, finely chopped
1 tablespoon ground cumin
1 tablespoon ground coriander
1 tablespoon smoked paprika
1 tablespoon chipotle chilli/chile paste (or 1½ teaspoons dried chilli/hot red pepper flakes)
1½ teaspoons sea salt
100 ml/⅓ cup cider vinegar
5 x 400-g/14-oz. cans chopped tomatoes

TO SERVE
12 eggs
550 g/1¼ lbs. pulled pork (see above)
6 slices of toasted sourdough
120 g/1½ cups very finely grated Parmesan cheese
15 g/1 cup coriander/cilantro leaves
freshly ground black pepper

SERVES 6

This dish is our version of Huevos Ahogados, a Mexican breakfast, which translates as 'drowned eggs' because the eggs are smothered in the spicy tomato sauce.

Preheat the oven to 220°C (425°F) Gas 7.

Mix all the marinade ingredients together in a bowl. With a sharp knife, make slashes all over the pork. Rub the marinade over the pork, making sure it gets into all the slashes. Put the pork into a baking dish with 250 ml/1 cup of water. Cover tightly with foil. Put the pork in the preheated oven for 30 minutes. Reduce the oven temperature to 110°C (225°F) Gas ¼ and leave to cook overnight or for at least 10 hours.

Remove the pork from the baking dish, reserving the liquor, and allow the meat to cool. Once cool enough to handle, remove and discard the skin and shred the meat into a bowl. Mix some of the reserved liquor back through the meat to keep it moist. You can store it in the fridge, covered, for up to a couple of days.

To make the tomato sauce, put the oil into a pan. Add the onions and garlic and cook over a low heat for 5–10 minutes until soft. Add the cumin, coriander, paprika, chilli/chile paste (or flakes) and salt and cook for a further 3 minutes, until fragrant.

Add the vinegar and deglaze the pan (remove any sticky bits from the bottom of the pan with a wooden spoon) before adding the canned tomatoes. Simmer gently for 1½ hours, uncovered, stirring occasionally with a spoon, until the sauce has reduced and is nice and thick.

When ready to serve, in a large frying pan/skillet, heat a little oil and fry the eggs in batches, transferring them to a large plate when cooked. Increase the heat to medium-high and wfry the shredded pork until crispy.

Put two fried eggs on each piece of toast, smother the eggs with generous spoonfuls of the tomato sauce, lay the crispy pulled pork on top of the sauce and add some Parmesan cheese. Garnish with coriander/cilantro leaves and black pepper. Serve.

PANCAKES WITH BANANA, SALTED CARAMEL & TOASTED PECANS

I have always preferred these light and delicate French-style pancakes to the thick and fluffy American ones. These are delicious stuffed with an endless variety of sweet or savoury fillings, but if I had to pick one, it's hard to beat the combination of bitter sweet salty caramel with banana and a crunch of nuts for texture.

PANCAKES
30 g/2 tablespoons butter, plus extra melted butter for cooking
100 g/³/₄ cup plain/all-purpose flour
1 tablespoon caster/granulated sugar
a pinch of salt
1 large egg
1 egg yolk
350 ml/scant 1¹/₂ cups milk

SALTED CARAMEL SAUCE
200 g/1 cup caster/granulated sugar
90 g/3 oz. butter
120 ml/¹/₂ cup single/light cream
¹/₂ teaspoon sea salt flakes, plus extra to serve

FILLING
2 bananas, peeled and sliced
100 g/³/₄ cup toasted pecans, crushed

SERVES 6

To make the pancakes, melt the butter in a small saucepan and set aside. Sift the flour into a large bowl and add the sugar and a pinch of salt.

In a separate bowl, lightly beat the egg and egg yolk and stir together with the milk and the cooled melted butter. Pour this mixture into the flour and whisk together until smooth.

Heat a small frying pan/skillet over a medium heat and brush with extra melted butter. Using a small ladle or a 125-ml/¹/₂-cup measuring cup, pour some batter into the pan, swirling the batter around the pan so it just covers the base. Cook for a minute or so, until the edges of the pancake begin to brown and the underside is golden. Slide a spatula underneath and gently flip the pancake over to cook on the other side for 30 seconds. Lift it out and set aside. Repeat the process until all the batter is used up. Cover the pancakes with foil to keep them warm.

To make the Salted Caramel Sauce, melt the sugar in a small pan over a medium heat, stirring continuously with a rubber spatula (don't use metal or the sugar may crystallize). Once the sugar has liquefied and turned a rich caramel colour, remove from the heat and add the butter and salt, mixing until well incorporated. Place the saucepan back onto a low heat and pour in the cream. It will bubble up. Beat it well until it's glossy and smooth (about 30 seconds) and then take it off the heat.

To assemble the pancakes, put a few slices of banana and some crushed toasted pecans on to each pancake and then fold into a triangle and drizzle well with the Salted Caramel Sauce. Sprinkle with extra sea salt and serve.

CONFIT DUCK & SWEET POTATO HASH
WITH KALE, HOT SAUCE & LEMON CRÈME FRAÎCHE

It might seem like an extravagant dish for breakfast but the richness of the confit duck is cut with the spicy hot sauce and the sweet potato. If preparing the duck seems too time-consuming, you can buy prepared confit duck legs from specialty delicatessens.

2 duck legs
40 g/2 ¹/₂ tablespoons rock salt
1 star anise, broken into pieces using a pestle and mortar
1 garlic clove, sliced
350 ml/scant 1 ¹/₂ cups duck fat or vegetable oil
1 bay leaf
1 sweet potato (approx. 350 g/ 12 oz.), scrubbed but not peeled
2 tablespoons olive oil
¹/₂ teaspoon nigella seeds
2 stalks (50 g/2 oz.) kale
50 g/3 ¹/₂ tablespoons crème fraîche
1 tablespoon freshly squeezed lemon juice
¹/₄ teaspoon sea salt
2 spring onions/scallions
2 eggs
sriracha hot sauce, to drizzle
leaves from 2 sprigs of coriander/ cilantro, freshly chopped

a baking sheet, lined with baking parchment

SERVES 2

Lay the duck legs in a shallow bowl or dish and rub all over with the rock salt, star anise pieces and garlic. Cover the dish with clingfilm/ plastic wrap and leave to marinate overnight (for approx. 12 hours) in the fridge.

Remove the duck legs from the bowl or dish and rinse off the salt. Pat dry with paper towels.

Preheat the oven to 110°C (225°F) Gas ¹/₄. Put the duck legs in a small roasting pan that fits them snugly and pour over the duck fat or vegetable oil so that the legs are completely covered. Add the bay leaf. Cover with a piece of baking parchment cut to fit the pan and then cover the dish with a double layer of foil. Cook in the preheated oven for 2¹/₂–3 hours or until the meat easily pulls away from the bone.

With a slotted spoon, lift the legs out of the oil and remove the excess fat from the duck with some paper towels. (You can reserve the fat/oil to use again in another recipe or discard it.) Shred the meat from the bone into large chunks, discarding the skin and bones.

For the roasted sweet potatoes, preheat the oven to 180°C (350°F) Gas 4.

Cut the scrubbed sweet potato into 2-cm/³/₄-inch cubes. Toss them with a tablespoon of the olive oil and the nigella seeds and place on the prepared baking sheet. Roast in the preheated oven for 15–20 minutes, until starting to colour and a knife inserts easily. Remove from the oven.

For the blanched kale, strip the kale leaves from the stalks and tear the leaves into bite-sized pieces. Place the leaves in a colander in the sink and then pour boiling water from the kettle over the kale so that the water drains straight off. When it is cool enough to handle, squeeze any excess water from the kale.

In a small bowl, mix the crème fraîche with the lemon juice and salt.

When ready to serve, heat the remaining olive oil in a large frying pan/skillet and when the oil is hot, add the sweet potato and shredded duck. Fry until they go a little crispy, then add the kale and spring onions/scallions and toss together in the pan for a minute. In another pan, fry the eggs in oil. Place the fried eggs on top of the hash. Drizzle with some sriracha sauce and sprinkle chopped coriander/cilantro on top. Either drizzle with the lemon crème fraîche or serve it on the side.

BUBBLE & SQUEAK

Bubble and squeak is a classic breakfast invention that transforms left over roast vegetables for the ultimate fry-up.

30 g/2 tablespoons unsalted butter
150 g/1 cup (about 1 medium) sliced onion
1 garlic clove, finely chopped
220 g/3½ cups (about ¼) shredded white cabbage
400 g/2 cups cold mashed potato
500 g/2½ cups cold roast vegetables (squash, carrot and parsnip)
15 g/¼ cup flat-leaf parsley, freshly chopped
sea salt and freshly ground black pepper

TO SERVE
black pudding, thickly sliced and grilled
4 fried eggs
Pear & Apple Chutney (see page 126)

SERVES 4

Melt the butter in a non-stick frying pan/skillet set over a low-medium heat. Add the onion and garlic and cook for about 10 minutes, until soft and caramelized.

Add the shredded cabbage and sweat down for 2–3 minutes. Add the mashed potato, roast vegetables, parsley and salt and pepper, and mix well. Cook for a further 15–20 minutes, turning the vegetables from time to time and using a spatula to flatten the vegetables onto the base of the pan so that they catch and get a crispy bottom.

Serve each portion with thick slices of grilled black pudding, a fried egg and some Pear & Apple Chutney.

CHORIZO, RED PEPPER & PEA FRITTATA BITES

A frittata is a baked omelette that is delicious at any time of the day, served hot or cold. We often make one for the breakfast counter at the café, cut into wedges for our takeaway customers.

4 x 60-g/2¼-oz. chorizo sausages
16 eggs
300 ml/1¼ cups crème fraîche
a pinch each of sea salt and freshly ground black pepper
1 tablespoon olive oil
150 g/1 cup (about 1 medium) finely chopped red onion
1 garlic clove, crushed
130 g/1 cup fresh (podded) or frozen peas
1 red (bell) pepper, deseeded and cut into strips
60 g/1¼ cups baby spinach

SERVES 8–10

Preheat the oven to 180°C (350°F) Gas 4.

Place the chorizo sausages on a baking sheet and cook in the preheated oven for 12 minutes. Remove from the oven, drain on paper towels and cut into 1-cm/½-inch slices. Cover and set aside.

Reduce the oven temperature to 150°C (300°F) Gas 2.

Put the eggs in a large mixing bowl with the crème fraîche and lightly whisk to combine. Season with the salt and pepper; set aside.

Heat the oil in a large, non-stick, ovenproof frying pan/skillet set over a low-medium heat. Add the onion and garlic and sauté until soft but not coloured.

Add the sliced chorizo, peas and red (bell) pepper strips and cook for 2–3 minutes, stirring occasionally. Add the baby spinach and stir until the spinach just begins to wilt.

Arrange the mix evenly over the base of the pan and carefully pour in the egg mixture.

Reduce the heat and gently cook the frittata, moving the egg in a little from the edge of the pan as it cooks (similar to how you would cook an omelette) using a spatula to run around the outside of the pan. You don't want to get any colour on the base of the frittata, so it is important to keep the temperature low.

Continue running the spatula around the outside of the pan to ensure the frittata doesn't stick. After about 10 minutes, once it has just set on the bottom and the sides, place the pan in the preheated oven for 15–20 minutes, until the frittata is lightly golden and just set in the middle. Remove from the oven and set aside to cool for 10 minutes.

Once cool, cover the pan with a chopping board and turn it over to release the frittata. Cut it into 4-cm/1½-inch squares and transfer to a plate to serve.

SAUSAGE & EGG MUFFINS WITH SMOKED CHEDDAR, WILTED SPINACH & SRIRACHA HOLLANDAISE

When I opened Lantana I made a bold claim that I would never put eggs benedict on the menu as I felt it was served in every café and I wanted to be different. After a few years of gentle, but persistent pressure, I relented and this twist became one of our best sellers.

4 good-quality Lincolnshire or Cumberland sausages (approximately 85 g/3 oz. each)
1 tablespoon olive oil
100 g/3 1/2 oz. Applewood smoked Cheddar cheese, sliced (4 square slices)
a knob of butter, plus extra for buttering the muffins
150 g/5 1/2 oz. baby spinach
4 English muffins
4 eggs, fried, over easy
sea salt and freshly ground black pepper

SRIRACHA HOLLANDAISE
150 g/1 1/4 sticks unsalted butter
2 egg yolks
1/2 teaspoon apple cider vinegar
1 teaspoon freshly squeezed lemon juice
1 tablespoon sriracha hot sauce

a baking sheet, lined with baking parchment

SERVES 4

For the hollandaise, melt the butter in a small pan over a low heat. Remove from the heat and skim the white solids off the surface with a spoon and discard. Put the egg yolks, vinegar and 2 teaspoons of cold water in a heatproof bowl and sit the bowl on top of a saucepan of barely simmering water. Make sure the base of the bowl does not touch the water. Using a metal whisk or hand-held blender, beat the egg yolks until they lighten in colour and double in volume.

Remove the saucepan from the heat, but keep the bowl over the saucepan, and slowly add the melted butter in a steady trickle, whisking or beating constantly. Once all the butter has been added and it has reached a mayonnaise-like consistency, stop whisking and stir in the lemon juice, sriracha sauce and salt to taste. Keep the hollandaise somewhere warm with a piece of clingfilm/plastic wrap touching the surface to stop a skin forming.

Preheat the oven to 160°C (325°F) Gas 3.

Remove the casing from the sausages and shape the sausagemeat filling into four flat round patties. In a frying pan/skillet, heat the olive oil over a medium heat and fry the sausage patties on both sides until lightly browned and cooked. Place on the prepared baking sheet, top each patty with a slice of smoked cheese and place in the preheated oven for a couple of minutes until the cheese has melted. Return the frying pan/skillet to the heat. Melt a knob of butter in the pan, then add the spinach and toss until it is just wilted. Season with salt and pepper and transfer to a bowl.

Slice the muffins in half horizontally and lightly toast. Butter both insides. To assemble, put the muffin bottoms on four serving plates, sit a sausage patty with the melted cheese on top of each, then some wilted spinach, then a fried egg, and spoon some hollandaise on top. Put the other halves of the muffins on top and serve.

BRUNCH PLATES & MAINS

BAKED RICOTTA WITH AUBERGINE, CURRANT & PINE NUT RELISH

Cheese and fruit is such a classic pairing, I think this irresistible relish works really well with the baked ricotta for brunch.

1 kg/5 cups ricotta
1 garlic clove, peeled
1/2 teaspoon sea salt
2 eggs, separated
1 teaspoon grated lemon zest
1 tablespoon thyme leaves
60 g/1 cup finely grated
   Parmesan cheese

RELISH
800 g/6 cups (about 2 large)
   diced aubergines/eggplants
125 ml/1/2 cup red wine
250 ml/1 cup balsamic vinegar
1/2 star anise
1 tablespoon caster/granulated
   sugar
125 ml/1/2 cup sunflower oil
1 tablespoon currants
3 tablespoons pine nuts/kernels,
   toasted
2 tablespoons freshly chopped
   flat-leaf parsley
sea salt and freshly ground
   black pepper

6 x 250-ml/1-cup capacity
   ramekins, greased

SERVES 6

Preheat the oven to 200°C (400°F) Gas 6.

Drain the ricotta in a fine mesh sieve/strainer and put in a large mixing bowl. Pound the garlic with the salt using a pestle and mortar. Stir the garlic paste through the ricotta together with the egg yolks, lemon zest, thyme and grated Parmesan.

In a separate large mixing bowl, whisk the egg whites to soft peaks. Add a large spoonful of the egg whites to the ricotta mixture and stir to loosen it. Gently fold in the remaining egg whites until just incorporated, then pour the mixture into the prepared ramekins.

Bake in the preheated oven for 20 minutes, until slightly golden on top and the cheese is just set. It will puff up slightly during cooking and deflate while cooling, so don't be alarmed. Allow the ricotta to cool completely before turning out onto serving plates.

Next, make the relish. Put the aubergine/eggplant in a large sieve/strainer set over a mixing bowl, cover with salt and set aside for 20 minutes. Rinse, pat dry and set aside. Place the red wine, balsamic vinegar, star anise and sugar in a medium saucepan or pot set over a medium heat. Bring to the boil, then reduce the heat and simmer for about 15 minutes, until the liquid has reduced by two-thirds and become syrupy.

Meanwhile, heat some of the oil in a large frying pan/skillet over a medium heat. Shallow-fry the aubergine/eggplant in batches until golden brown. Add extra oil as required. Drain the aubergine/eggplant on paper towels and set aside.

Remove the star anise from the red wine reduction. Add the currants and fried aubergine/eggplant, and simmer gently over a low heat with a lid on for 30 minutes – most of the liquid should be soaked up. Remove from the heat and stir in the pine nuts/kernels and parsley. Season to taste and serve with the ricotta.

CAPONATA WITH GRILLED POLENTA & WHIPPED FETA

**700 g/7 cups (about 2) diced
aubergines/eggplants**
125 ml/½ cup olive oil
1 large onion, diced
1 garlic clove, crushed
**1 red plus 1 orange or yellow (bell)
pepper, deseeded and diced**
**2 celery stalks, cut on an angle
into 2-cm/¾-inch slices**
4 tablespoons red wine vinegar
**1 x 400-g/14-oz. can chopped
tomatoes**
**2 teaspoons caster/ granulated
sugar**
**35 g/⅓ cup green olives, pitted
and halved**
**1 tablespoon capers, rinsed
and drained**
**20 g/¼ cup flaked/slivered
almonds, lightly toasted**
**sea salt and freshly ground
black pepper**
**a handful of freshly chopped
flat-leaf parsley, to serve**

GRILLED POLENTA

**200 g/1⅓ cups quick-cook
polenta/cornmeal**
80 g/5 tablespoons butter
**50 g/1 cup grated Parmesan
cheese**

WHIPPED FETA

250 g/2 cups feta cheese
60 ml/¼ cup Greek yogurt
60 ml/¼ cup extra virgin olive oil
**1 tablespoon freshly squeezed
lemon juice**

*an 18 x 25-cm/7 x 10-inch
baking pan, greased*
a baking sheet, oiled

SERVES 6

Caponata improves with age and is extremely versatile.
It makes a great vegetarian dish, served here with polenta.

Put the aubergine/eggplant in a colander and sprinkle with salt.
Leave for 30 minutes then rinse under cold, running water and
pat dry with paper towels.

Heat the oil in a large, heavy-bottomed saucepan over a medium
heat. Add the aubergine/eggplant and fry for 5–8 minutes, until
golden brown, stirring occasionally. Remove from the pan and set
aside. Add the onion to the same pan and fry for 5 minutes, or
until softened. You may need to add a little more oil. Add the garlic
and cook for another minute before adding the peppers and celery.
Cook for 5 minutes, then add the vinegar and stir to deglaze the
pan. Stir in the tomatoes and sugar and simmer for 5–10 minutes.

Return the aubergine/eggplant to the pan with the olives and
capers, and mix well. Cook for a further 5 minutes. Remove from
the heat, season and stir in the almonds.

To make the polenta, bring 1 litre/4 cups of salted water to the boil
in a medium saucepan or pot. Gradually pour in the polenta while
stirring continuously with a wooden spoon. Reduce the heat and
keep stirring for about 5 minutes. Remove from the heat and stir
in the butter and the Parmesan. Adjust the seasoning as necessary.
Working quickly, spread the polenta mix evenly across the prepared
baking pan to a layer 2 cm/¾ inch deep. Set aside to cool.

For the Whipped Feta, crumble the feta into a food processor and
pulse together with the yogurt until smooth. Add the oil and mix
until it becomes very soft. Add the lemon juice and put in the fridge.

Preheat a grill/broiler to a medium heat. Tip the set polenta onto
a board and cut into six rectangles. Cut these in half diagonally
to give you 12 triangles. Place the polenta on the prepared baking
sheet and set under the grill/broiler to cook for about 10 minutes,
or until golden. Turn the polenta and grill the other side in the
same way. Reheat the caponata over a medium heat, add the
parsley and stir through. Heap the caponata onto plates, top with
the Grilled Polenta and a dollop of Whipped Feta. Season and serve.

SLOW-BRAISED BEANS WITH HAM HOCK

You need to start this recipe a day in advance – the beans need to soak overnight and the ham hock can take up to 5 hours to cook. It's worth the wait though and Cheddar Cornbread (page 102) is the ideal accompaniment.

500 g/1 1/2 cups dried cannellini beans
1 1/2 teaspoons fennel seeds
1 x 2-kg/4 1/2-lbs. ham hock
1 red (bell) pepper
2 tablespoons olive oil
1 onion, finely diced
2 garlic cloves, finely grated
2 x 400-g/14-oz. cans chopped tomatoes
1 1/2 teaspoons dried chilli/hot red pepper flakes
1 1/2 teaspoons sweet smoked paprika
500 ml/2 cups vegetable stock
75 ml/1/4 cup black treacle/ molasses
50 g/3 tablespoons tomato purée/ paste
50 ml/2 fl oz. Worcestershire sauce
2 bay leaves
1 star anise
1 1/2 teaspoons English mustard powder
a sprig of rosemary, roughly chopped
sea salt and freshly ground black pepper

a baking sheet lined with foil

SERVES 6–8

Soak the dried cannellini beans in water overnight, then rinse and discard the water.

Place the soaked beans, fennel seeds and ham hock in a large saucepan or pot and cover with cold water. Set over a medium-high heat and bring to the boil. Reduce the heat and simmer gently for about 45 minutes, until just soft. Drain, discard the water and reserve the beans, seeds and ham hock. Cover and set aside.

Preheat the oven to 200°C (400°F) Gas 6.

Place the (bell) pepper on the prepared baking sheet and roast in the preheated oven for 20 minutes. Turn and roast for another 20 minutes, until the skin is blackened in most parts and the (bell) pepper collapses. Remove from oven and reduce the heat to 140°C (275°F) Gas 1. Put the (bell) pepper in a bowl, cover with clingfilm/ plastic wrap and set aside for 10 minutes. Once it is cool enough to handle, remove the skin, core and seeds, then dice the flesh.

Heat the olive oil in a frying pan/skillet set over a medium heat and sweat the onion until soft. Add the garlic and continue to cook for 1 minute before transferring to a large, shallow, ovenproof casserole dish. Add the drained, cooked beans and seeds, the chopped tomatoes, roasted (bell) pepper, dried chilli/hot red pepper flakes, paprika, vegetable stock, black treacle/molasses, tomato purée/paste, Worcestershire sauce, bay leaves, star anise, mustard powder and rosemary. Gently mix together.

Nestle the ham hock into the beans, cover with foil and cook in the oven for 3 hours. After this time, remove the foil and cook for another 1–2 hours, until the ham hock is cooked – the meat is cooked when it is easy to pull away from the bone.

Remove the dish from the oven and transfer the ham hock to a large plate to cool slightly. When it is cool enough to handle, cut off the skin and fat and discard. Shred the meat, then return it to the casserole dish with the beans. Stir well, season and serve.

BUTTERNUT SQUASH, EGG, CRISPY CAVOLO NERO, FETA, POMEGRANATE SEEDS & JALAPEÑO ZHOUG

500 g/1 lb. 2 oz. peeled and deseeded butternut squash, cut into 2.5-cm/1-inch chunks
1 tablespoon olive oil, plus extra for roasting the butternut squash and cavolo nero
2 small garlic cloves, crushed
1 teaspoon thyme leaves
30 g/3 tablespoons whole almonds, toasted and roughly chopped
a few sprigs of mint, leaves roughly chopped
1 teaspoon pomegranate molasses
6 stems cavolo nero (approx. 70 g/2½ oz.), stalks removed, chopped into 2.5-cm/1-inch pieces
2 slices of focaccia or pitta bread
2 eggs
50 g/⅓ cup feta cheese, crumbled
1–2 tablespoons pomegranate seeds
sea salt and freshly ground black pepper

JALAPENO ZHOUG
65 g/3 cups coriander/cilantro, leaves and stalks chopped
30 g/½ cup jalapeño or green chillies/chiles, chopped
1 teaspoon sea salt
1 garlic clove, chopped
200 ml/¾ cup olive oil
20 ml/1 tablespoon plus 1 teaspoon freshly squeezed lemon juice

2 baking sheets lined with baking parchment

SERVES 2

When the demand for avocados became so high that we literally couldn't source enough for the restaurant, we started serving this dish as an alternative. Like avocado, butternut squash provides a great backdrop for contrasting textures, colours and flavours. It offers a seasonal treat and a respite from 'avo overload'.

Preheat the oven to 180°C (350°F) Gas 4.

Spread the butternut squash chunks out on a prepared baking sheet, drizzle with olive oil, season with salt and pepper and roast in the preheated oven for about 20 minutes or until tender.

Remove from the oven, transfer to a bowl and mash roughly with a fork, keeping it a bit chunky.

Heat 1 tablespoon olive oil in a small pan, add the crushed garlic and thyme leaves and cook over a gentle heat for a couple of minutes. Add this to the smashed butternut squash with the chopped almonds, mint and pomegranate molasses. Season with salt and pepper.

Put the cavolo nero in a bowl, drizzle with olive oil and season with salt and pepper. Gently rub the oil into the cavolo nero leaves with your fingers and spread it out on the second prepared baking sheet. Roast on the top shelf of the preheated oven for about 5 minutes, until crispy.

To make the Jalapeño Zhoug, put all the ingredients in a food processor and blitz to a paste.

When ready to serve, gently reheat the smashed butternut squash in a pan. Toast the focaccia or pitta bread and poach the eggs.

Heap the smashed butternut squash on two plates, top with the crumbled feta, cavolo nero and pomegranate seeds. Serve with a generous dollop of Zhoug, the toasted focaccia and a poached egg.

CAULIFLOWER CAKES

1 tablespoon olive oil
320 g/4 cups cauliflower florets, diced into small pieces
1 garlic clove, finely chopped
240 g/8½ oz. canned chickpeas, drained and rinsed
½ tablespoon smoked paprika
½ teaspoon ground cumin
½ teaspoon cayenne pepper
½ teaspoon sea salt
2 spring onions/scallions (stems removed), chopped
100 g/¾ cup pumpkin seeds
20 g/1 cup freshly chopped parsley
40 g/¼ cup gluten-free or chickpea/gram flour
1 tablespoon flaxseeds/linseeds

baking sheet lined with baking parchment, drizzled with oil

MAKES 18 CAKES

MUHAMMARA

3 red (bell) peppers
1 tablespoon freshly squeezed lemon juice
1 tablespoon pomegranate molasses
1 teaspoon ground cumin
1 tablespoon dried chilli/hot red pepper flakes
½ garlic clove, peeled
100 g/1 cup walnuts, chopped
½ teaspoon sea salt
60 ml/¼ cup olive oil

SERVES 4

PICKLED RED ONION

200 ml/¾ cup white wine vinegar
5 teaspoons sea salt
100 g/½ cup caster/granulated sugar
1 red onion, halved and thinly sliced

SERVES 4

NOURISH BOWLS WITH CAULIFLOWER CAKES, MUHAMMARA, COURGETTE & BEETROOT SALAD & PICKLED RED ONION

We've seen a huge increase in demand for plant-based dishes on our menu. Nourish bowls are the answer to this calling, but far from being dull and worthy, their kaleidoscope of textures, tastes and colours makes for beautiful bowls of flavour.

To make the Cauliflower Cakes, heat the olive oil in a large frying pan/skillet and fry the cauliflower with the garlic, chickpeas, spices and salt. Cook for 4–5 minutes over a medium heat, coating the chickpeas and cauliflower with the seasoning and oil. Remove from the pan and place the mixture in a food processor with the spring onions/scallions, half the pumpkin seeds and the parsley. Blend until it is all mixed, scraping the sides and mixing again, until it holds together. Transfer to a mixing bowl and stir in the flour and the remaining pumpkin seeds and flaxseeds/linseeds. Chill the batter for 10 minutes in the fridge to firm up a little and then form into round patties roughly 40 g/1½ oz. each.

Preheat the oven to 180°C (350°F) Gas 4. Place the patties on the prepared baking sheet and brush the tops with oil. Bake in the preheated oven for 10–15 minutes, flipping once, until lightly browned on both sides. Remove from the oven and cool.

To make the Muhammara, preheat the oven to 180°C (350°F) Gas 4. Roast the (bell) peppers on a baking sheet in the preheated oven for 30 minutes until the skins blacken. Remove the (bell) peppers from the oven, put in a bowl and cover with a plate. When cool, remove the skin and seeds. Put the (bell) peppers into a blender with all the remaining ingredients and blitz to a rough paste.

For the Pickled Red Onion, put the vinegar, salt and sugar into a medium saucepan and gently heat to dissolve the sugar and salt. Remove from the heat, cool the liquid and then pour over the sliced onions in a bowl.

- 1 medium courgette/zucchini, spiralized or thinly sliced
- 1 medium beetroot/beet, peeled and spiralized or thinly sliced
- 4 tablespoons freshly chopped mint
- 2 tablespoons freshly chopped flat-leaf parsley
- 1 tablespoon freshly squeezed lemon juice
- 2 tablespoons olive oil
- $1/2$ teaspoon sea salt
- 200 g/7 oz. Muhammara (see left)
- 12 x Cauliflower Cakes (see left)
- 85 g/3 oz. Pickled Red Onion (see left)
- $1/2$ cucumber, thinly sliced
- 50 g/$1/3$ cup blanched whole almonds, toasted

SERVES 4

Put the courgette/zucchini and beetroot/beet spirals into a large bowl and add the chopped herbs. Mix together the lemon juice, olive oil and salt and toss over the vegetables and herbs.

Divide the salad between four serving bowls, arranging it to one side of the bowls. On the other side of the bowls, put a generous amount (3 tablespoons) of the Muhammara and sit the Cauliflower Cakes on top.

Take the Pickled Red Onion out of its brine, squeezing out any excess liquid. Toss the cucumber with the pickled red onion and place some of this salad to the side of the cakes in each bowl. Depending on what look you are going for, arrange the nuts in a line across the bowl, cluster them to one side, or sprinkle over the top.

CORN FRITTERS WITH ROAST TOMATOES & SMASHED AVOCADOS

Corn fritters are a menu staple in nearly every café in Australia and New Zealand. No two recipes are ever the same, as everyone has their (strong!) opinion on what makes the perfect fritter.

150 g/2 cups (about 1 medium) grated courgette/zucchini
400 g/2½ cups cherry vine tomatoes
olive oil, to drizzle
4 eggs
180 g/1⅓ cups self-raising/rising flour
50 g/1¾ oz. Parmesan cheese, grated
100 ml/scant ½ cup buttermilk
1 teaspoon paprika
½ teaspoon cayenne pepper
1 tablespoon freshly chopped coriander/cilantro
fresh corn kernels cut from 2–3 cobs
sea salt and freshly ground black pepper
sunflower oil, for frying

SMASHED AVOCADOS
3 avocados
grated zest of 1 lime and freshly squeezed juice of 2
¼ red onion, finely diced
1 teaspoon hot sauce

TO SERVE
fresh spinach leaves
crème fraîche

SERVES 6

Put the grated courgette/zucchini into a colander set over a large mixing bowl. Sprinkle with ½ teaspoon of salt and leave for 30 minutes–1 hour so they release their moisture. Squeeze the grated courgette/zucchini with your hands to get rid of as much moisture as possible and set aside.

For the roast tomatoes, preheat the oven to 180°C (350°F) Gas 4. Place the tomatoes on a baking sheet, drizzle with olive oil and season with salt and pepper.

Roast in the preheated oven for 15–20 minutes, or until the skins begin to split.

Reduce the oven temperature to 170°C (325°F) Gas 3 and prepare the fritter batter. In a large, clean, mixing bowl, lightly whisk the eggs. Add in the flour, grated Parmesan, buttermilk, paprika, cayenne pepper, ½ teaspoon of salt, a pinch of pepper and the chopped coriander/cilantro.

Stir in the squeezed courgette/zucchini and the corn kernels, ensuring the vegetables are evenly coated in batter.

Add enough sunflower oil to thinly cover the bottom of a heavy-bottomed frying pan/skillet. Ladle generous spoonfuls of batter into the pan and cook for about 4 minutes on each side, until golden brown. Transfer to a clean baking sheet and put in the oven for 4–5 minutes to ensure they are cooked through. Cook the remaining batter in the same way, adding a little more oil to the pan each time, if required.

Just before serving, roughly mash the avocados with a fork, leaving them fairly chunky. Stir in the lime zest and juice, onion and hot sauce. Season generously with salt and serve with the fritters, roast tomatoes, a handful of baby spinach and a dollop of crème fraîche.

SAUTÉED MIXED MUSHROOMS WITH
LEMON HERBED FETA ON TOASTED SOURDOUGH

This dish is inspired by the mushroom stall on Broadway market in London where they make amazing fried mushroom sandwiches for queues of hungry customers every Saturday. If a stall holder can pump out sandwiches this good using a single frying pan/skillet in the outdoors come wind, rain or snow, it seems the perfect quick dish for a small, busy café.

60 g/½ cup feta cheese
¼ teaspoon grated lemon zest
1 tablespoon flat-leaf parsley, roughly chopped
2 sprigs of thyme, roughly chopped
2 teaspoons olive oil, plus 1 tablespoon for frying
30 g/2 tablespoons butter
400 g/6 cups mixed mushrooms (chestnut, flat, button, oyster), thickly sliced
1 garlic clove, crushed
sea salt and freshly ground black pepper
60 g/generous 1 cup spinach
4 slices of sourdough bread

SERVES 2

Begin by making the herbed feta. Crumble the feta into a small mixing bowl. Add the lemon zest, parsley, thyme and 2 teaspoons of olive oil. Mash gently with a fork to combine and set aside.

To sauté the mushrooms, melt the butter and remaining 1 tablespoon of olive oil in a frying pan/skillet set over a high heat. Get the pan really hot without burning the butter before adding the mushrooms and garlic. Toss in the pan for a few minutes to coat the mushrooms, until they start to brown and crisp at the edges. Add a couple of good pinches of salt and pepper and allow the liquid in the mushrooms to evaporate, tossing the pan from time to time.

Add the spinach, stir through and remove the pan from the heat as it just starts to wilt. It will continue to cook from the heat of the mushrooms.

Toast the bread and pile each slice generously with the mushrooms and spinach. Crumble the herbed feta on top and serve.

CORN FRITTER BLINIS
WITH SMOKED SALMON & LEMON CREAM

Corn gives these blinis a slight twist on the traditional smoked salmon blinis. The blinis can be made ahead of time but assemble just before serving.

225 g/2 cups (about 1 medium) grated courgette/zucchini
4 eggs
180 g/1⅓ cups self-raising/ rising flour
50 g/1¾ oz. Parmesan cheese, grated
100 ml/scant ½ cup buttermilk
1 teaspoon paprika
½ teaspoon cayenne pepper
1 tablespoon freshly chopped coriander/cilantro
fresh corn kernels cut from 2–3 cobs
sunflower oil, for frying
sea salt and freshly ground black pepper
300 g/1½ cups smoked salmon, to serve
chervil or chopped chives, to garnish

LEMON CREAM
250 ml/1 cup sour/soured cream
1 tablespoon freshly squeezed lemon juice
1 teaspoon grated lemon zest
¼ teaspoon sea salt

MAKES 30–35 AND SERVES 10–15

Put the grated courgette/zucchini into a colander set over a large mixing bowl. Sprinkle with ½ teaspoon of salt and leave for 30 minutes–1 hour so they release their moisture. Squeeze the grated courgette/zucchini with your hands to get rid of as much moisture as possible and set aside.

In a large, clean mixing bowl, lightly whisk the eggs. Add the flour, grated Parmesan, buttermilk, paprika, cayenne pepper, ½ teaspoon of salt, a little pepper and the chopped coriander/ cilantro.

Stir in the squeezed courgette/zucchini and the corn kernels, ensuring the vegetables are evenly coated in batter.

Add enough sunflower oil to thinly cover the bottom of a heavy-bottomed frying pan/skillet. Drop small spoonfuls of batter into the pan using a teaspoon and cook for about 2 minutes on each side, until golden brown. Drain on paper towels, then transfer to a clean baking sheet. Cook the remaining batter in the same way, adding a little more oil to the pan each time, if required. If you are not going to assemble the blinis straight away, cool completely and cover with clingfilm/plastic wrap.

To make the Lemon Cream, combine the sour/soured cream, lemon juice and zest and salt in a small bowl.

Arrange the blinis on a serving platter, top with a ribbon of smoked salmon and a dollop of Lemon Cream. Garnish with chervil or chopped chives and a sprinkle of freshly ground black pepper.

CHEESE ON TOAST WITH KASOUNDI

Chutneys and preserves are the unsung heroes of the culinary world; always an accompaniment and never the star of the show. For me, they deserve centre stage. They lend themselves so beautifully to café food as they spice up the simplest of dishes – Kasoundi with melted cheese on toast, cornbread with chilli jam, or grilled black pudding with apple and pear compote. The beauty of making your own preserves is that you can make big batches at a time and fill your store cupboard with treasures that only improve with age.

3 slices of sourdough bread
150 g/1½ cups grated Cheddar cheese

KASOUNDI
5 x 5-cm/2-inch pieces of fresh ginger, peeled and finely chopped
1 bulb garlic, chopped
30 g/¼ cup (about 2) deseeded and chopped green chillies/chiles
250 ml/1 cup malt vinegar
70 ml/¼ cup vegetable oil
45 g/4½ tablespoons black mustard seeds
15 g/2 tablespoons ground turmeric
45 g/5 tablespoons ground cumin
20 g/3 tablespoons chilli/chili powder
1 kg/5 cups firm ripe tomatoes, chopped
30 g/6 teaspoons sea salt
125 g/½ cup soft brown sugar

sterilized glass jars with airtight lids

MAKES 1½ LITRES
   (54 FL. OZ.)/6 CUPS

SERVES 1

To make the Kasoundi, put the ginger, garlic and chillies/chiles with 25 ml/1½ tablespoons of the vinegar in a food processor and blend to a smooth paste.

Heat the oil in a heavy-bottomed saucepan or pot set over a medium heat. Add the mustard seeds, turmeric, cumin and chilli/chili powder. Stir and cook for about 4 minutes, taking care not to let the mixture stick to the bottom of the pan, blacken or burn.

Pour in the ginger paste and cook for a further 5 minutes. Add the tomatoes, salt, remaining vinegar and the sugar. Reduce the heat and simmer for 1–1½ hours, stirring occasionally to prevent sticking.

The Kasoundi is ready when it is thick and there is a trace of oil on top.

While still warm, spoon the Kasoundi into sterilized glass jars. Carefully tap them on the counter to get rid of any air pockets, wipe clean and tightly screw on the lids. The Kasoundi can be stored unopened in a cool, dark place for up to 6 months. Once opened, store in the fridge and use within 2 weeks.

For the cheese on toast, preheat the grill/broiler. Lightly toast the bread, then add the cheese. Return to the grill/broiler until melted and bubbling. Serve with a generous helping of Kasoundi on top.

SMASHED AVOCADO ON TOAST
WITH RAW COURGETTE & HERB SALAD & DUKKAH

Avocados continue to reign supreme in the world of brunch.
A version of this dish has always been a bestseller on our menu.
The nutty dukkah adds great texture and saltiness to counter-
balance the creaminess of the avocado and the courgette/
zucchini salad gives it a wonderful freshness.

2 ripe avocados

**1 tablespoon freshly squeezed
lemon juice**

**1 small courgette/zucchini
(approx. 100 g/3½ oz.)**

**15 g/½ oz. mixed fresh herb
leaves, such as mint, coriander/
cilantro and flat-leaf parsley**

2 teaspoons extra virgin olive oil

1 teaspoon grated lemon zest

**2 slices of sourdough bread,
toasted**

**2 tablespoons Dukkah
(see recipe on 28)**

**sea salt and freshly ground
black pepper**

SERVES 2

Cut the avocados in half, remove the stones and scoop out the flesh into a bowl. Roughly mash the flesh with a fork, keeping it quite chunky. Add the lemon juice with a generous pinch of sea salt and black pepper. Gently combine.

To make the courgette/zucchini salad, use a mandolin or vegetable peeler to slice the courgette/zucchini into long thin ribbons. Place into a bowl with the herb leaves, olive oil, lemon zest and a pinch of salt and pepper. Toss together.

Spread the smashed avocado generously onto the two slices of toast. Heap the courgette/zucchini salad on top and sprinkle with the Dukkah.

ASPARAGUS, GOAT'S CHEESE & SPINACH TART

I always like to be able to tell what flavour a tart is by looking at it. Here, with the asparagus floating on the surface like synchronized swimmers, there's no mistaking who's the star of the show.

90 g/6 tablespoons cold unsalted butter, cut into small pieces
180 g/1½ cups plain/all-purpose flour, plus extra for dusting
a pinch of sea salt
2–3 tablespoons ice-cold water

FILLING
7 eggs
250 ml/1 cup double/ heavy cream
200 g/¾ cup crème fraîche
150 g/1½ cups goat's cheese
80 g/1⅓ cups baby spinach leaves
12 asparagus spears, ends removed
sea salt and freshly ground black pepper

a 20-cm/8-inch round, deep, fluted tart pan
baking beans

SERVES 8–10

Preheat the oven to 190°C (375°F) Gas 5.

Place the butter, flour and salt in a food processor and pulse the mixture for 20–30 seconds, until it resembles coarse breadcrumbs. With the motor running, add the ice-cold water slowly and stop as soon as the dough comes together. It is important not to overmix the dough as it will become tough, and if you add too much water it will shrink as it cooks. Wrap the dough in clingfilm/plastic wrap and chill in the fridge for at least 30 minutes before using.

Roll the pastry out as thinly as possible on a lightly floured surface. Line the tart pan with the pastry and prick the base all over with a fork. Place on a baking sheet, line with a piece of greased baking parchment slightly larger than the pan and fill with baking beans.

Bake in the preheated oven for 15–20 minutes. Remove the baking beans and parchment and return the pastry case to the oven to cook for a further 5–10 minutes, or until it is pale golden and cooked through. Remove from the oven and set aside to cool. Reduce the oven temperature to 160°C (325°F) Gas 3.

For the filling, in a large mixing bowl, whisk together the eggs, cream and crème fraîche. Season with salt and pepper, then gently stir in the goat's cheese and spinach.

Pour the mixture into the cooled tart case, making sure the cheese and spinach are evenly distributed.

Lay the asparagus spears in a single layer on top of the egg mixture, alternating head and tail, and gently push them into the tart.

Bake in the oven for about 1 hour, until golden and just set. Serve hot or cold.

LEEK, ROCKET & PARMESAN TART

Every day on the takeaway counter we have a selection of lusciously creamy, freshly baked tarts. The fillings vary but this one is a trusted favourite. The recipe requires a deep pan as there is nothing more disappointing than a thin, mean-looking tart.

90 g/6 tablespoons cold unsalted butter, cut into small pieces
180 g/1/2 cups plain/all-purpose flour, plus extra for dusting
a pinch of sea salt
2–3 tablespoons ice-cold water

FILLING
20 g/4 teaspoons butter
2–3 leeks, trimmed and thinly sliced on the diagonal
7 eggs
250 ml/1 cup double/heavy cream
200 g/3/4 cup crème fraîche
130 g/1 2/3 cups grated Parmesan cheese
80 g/1 1/3 cups rocket/arugula
sea salt and freshly ground black pepper

a 20-cm/8-inch round, deep, fluted tart pan
baking beans

SERVES 8–10

Preheat the oven to 190°C (375°F) Gas 5.

Place the butter, flour and salt in a food processor and pulse the mixture for 20–30 seconds, until it resembles coarse breadcrumbs. With the motor running, add the ice-cold water slowly and stop as soon as the dough comes together. It is important not to over mix the dough as it will become tough and if you add too much water it will shrink as it cooks. Wrap the dough in clingfilm/plastic wrap and chill in the fridge for at least 30 minutes before using.

Roll the pastry out as thinly as possible on a lightly floured surface. Line the tart pan with the pastry and prick the base all over with a fork. Place the pan on a baking sheet, line with a piece of greased baking parchment slightly larger than the pan and fill the case with baking beans.

Bake in the preheated oven for 15–20 minutes. Remove the baking beans and parchment and return the pastry case to the oven to cook for a further 5–10 minutes, or until it is pale golden and cooked through. Remove from the oven and set aside to cool.

Reduce the oven temperature to 160°C (325°F) Gas 3.

Melt the butter in a large saucepan or pot set over a medium heat. Add the leeks and sweat until soft but avoid browning.

In a large mixing bowl, whisk together the eggs, cream and crème fraîche. Season with salt and pepper, then gently stir in the Parmesan, cooked leeks and rocket/arugula.

Pour the mixture into the cooled tart case, making sure the leeks and rocket/arugula are evenly distributed.

Bake in the oven for about 1 hour, until golden and just set. Serve hot or cold.

SANDWICHES & SALADS

3 tablespoons olive oil
115 g/¾ cup finely diced onion
3 garlic cloves, crushed
a 4-cm/1½-inch piece of fresh
    ginger, peeled and finely grated
900 g/2 lbs. minced/ground pork
2 long red chillies/chiles,
    deseeded and finely chopped
1 tablespoon fish sauce
2 tablespoons freshly chopped
    coriander/cilantro
60 g/2¼ oz. streaky bacon,
    chopped
2 eggs
sea salt and freshly ground
    black pepper

MANGO SALSA
2 mangoes, peeled, pitted and
    very finely diced
1 long red chilli/chile, deseeded
    and finely diced
1 tablespoon freshly chopped
    coriander/cilantro
1 tablespoon roughly chopped
    mint leaves
½ medium red onion, finely diced
freshly squeezed juice of 1 lime
2 teaspoons palm sugar/jaggery

FENNEL & MINT SLAW
2 heaped tablespoons mayonnaise
grated zest and freshly squeezed
    juice of 1 lemon
200 g/7 oz. (about 1 small) fennel
    bulb, trimmed, sliced into rings
a bunch of freshly chopped mint
40 g/scant 1 cup freshly chopped
    flat-leaf parsley
40 g/1½ oz. rocket/arugula
½ red onion, thinly sliced

TO SERVE
6 burger buns
mayonnaise

SERVES 6

SPICY PORK BURGERS
WITH MANGO SALSA

The spicy Asian flavours and sweet fresh mango salsa set this succulent pork burger apart from a traditional beef burger, and makes a lighter alternative too.

To make the Mango Salsa, mix all of the ingredients together in a bowl and set aside.

To make the Fennel & Mint Slaw, mix the mayonnaise with the lemon zest and juice and then dress the fennel straight away to prevent the fennel discolouring. Gently mix through the herbs, rocket/arugula and red onion. Set aside.

For the burgers, heat 1 tablespoon of the oil in a frying pan/skillet and sauté the onion, garlic and ginger over a gentle heat until soft. Remove from the heat and allow to cool.

Place all the remaining ingredients in a large bowl, add the onion mixture and combine. Season with salt and pepper.

Form the burger mixture into six burger patties (about 180 g/6¼ oz. each). Refrigerate until ready to cook.

Preheat the oven to 170°C (325°F) Gas 3.

Heat the remaining 2 tablespoons of oil in a large frying pan/skillet over a medium heat and fry the burger patties for 4 minutes, turning once, until nice and brown on both sides. You may need to do this in batches, depending on the size of your pan/skillet.

Transfer the burgers to a baking sheet and finish them off in the preheated oven for a further 10 minutes.

While the burgers are cooking, halve, then lightly toast the burger buns. Spread some mayonnaise on the bottom buns and top with the pork burgers, Mango Salsa and the other halves of the buns. Serve with the Fennel & Mint Slaw on the side.

2½ kg/5½ lbs. raw salt beef brisket, rinsed
150 g/1 cup (about 1 medium) quartered red onion
200 g/1½ cups (about 1 large) chopped carrot
100 g/¾ cup (about 2 stalks) celery, halved
6 garlic cloves
25 g/scant ½ cup rosemary needles
10 g/scant ¼ cup thyme leaves
3 bay leaves
1 teaspoon black peppercorns

PICKLING LIQUID
250 g/1¼ cups caster/ granulated sugar
500 ml/2 cups white wine vinegar
1 cinnamon stick
4 whole cloves
2 star anise
2 teaspoons coriander seeds
2 teaspoons fennel seeds
2 teaspoons black peppercorns

HOMEMADE PICKLES
450 g/4½ cups (about ½ small) finely shredded red cabbage
300 g/2½ cups (about 2 medium) julienne-sliced carrot
1 long red chilli/chile, deseeded and julienne-sliced
sea salt

TO SERVE
12–16 slices light rye bread
mustard mayonnaise
50 g/1 cup rocket/arugula
30 g/½ cup flat-leaf parsley leaves
1 teaspoon black onion seeds or ground fennel

sterilized glass jars with airtight lids

SERVES 6–8

BEEF BRISKET
WITH HOMEMADE PICKLES

We serve our brisket sandwich without a lid – it seems a shame to hide the glistening salt beef and beautiful pickles under a slice of bread. You can also serve it on a bagel.

Place the rinsed raw brisket in a large pot with the onion, carrot, celery, garlic, rosemary, thyme, bay leaves and peppercorns. Cover with fresh, cold water and set over a high heat.

Bring the water to the boil, then reduce the heat and simmer gently, covered with a lid, for 2–3 hours until the beef is cooked but still holding together. Remove the brisket from the stock and set aside to cool completely before slicing thinly, ensuring the cuts are made across the grain of the meat.

To make the Homemade Pickles, first prepare the Pickling Liquid. Place all the ingredients in a saucepan or pot with 125 ml/½ cup of water. Set over a medium-high heat and bring to the boil, stirring to ensure the sugar dissolves. Reduce the heat and simmer for 15 minutes, then remove from the heat, cover and set aside overnight to allow the flavours to infuse.

Toss the shredded cabbage in a good amount of salt in a bowl and place in the fridge overnight.

The next day, reheat the Pickling Liquid. Rinse the salted cabbage, then pat it dry with a clean kitchen towel. Mix with the sliced carrot and chilli/chile and place in sterilized glass jars. Pour over the hot pickling liquid so that the vegetables are completely submerged, then seal and store as per the recipe on page 62.

To serve, toast the rye bread and spread each slice generously with mustard mayonnaise. Place some rocket/arugula on the bread and layer the salt beef over the bread. Take the pickled vegetables out of their pickling liquid, drain on paper towels and place in a bowl with the parsley and black onion seeds or ground fennel. Toss to combine and place a small heap on top of each sandwich.

STEAK SANDWICHES WITH BEETROOT JAM & BLUE CHEESE DRESSING

Beetroot/beet and blue cheese is a classic combination, one that works really well with beef, which is strong enough to hold its own with these gutsy flavours. You could easily substitute burgers for the steak and serve them in a bun.

4 x 150-g/5½-oz. rump steaks
olive oil
8 slices of sourdough bread
80 g/1²/₃ cups watercress
2 large tomatoes, sliced

BEETROOT/BEET JAM/JELLY
500 g/3¼ cups roughly chopped
    beetroots/beets
50 g/4 tablespoons finely grated
    fresh horseradish
100 ml/¹/₃ cup balsamic vinegar
50 g/¼ cup light brown sugar
1 teaspoon sea salt

BLUE CHEESE DRESSING
60 g/¼ cup sour/soured cream
60 ml/¼ cup buttermilk
1 tablespoon freshly squeezed
    lemon juice
1 tablespoon freshly chopped dill
½ teaspoon sea salt
100 g/³/₄ cup crumbled Stilton
    or other blue cheese
freshly ground black pepper

SERVES 4

Begin by preparing the Beetroot/Beet Jam/Jelly. Put the beetroots/beets in a saucepan or pot of boiling water and cook for about 40 minutes, until just tender. Drain and set aside to cool.

Once cool enough to handle, peel and grate into a clean, large saucepan or pot.

Add all the other ingredients, set the pan over a gentle heat and simmer for 30–40 minutes until there is no liquid and the beetroots/beets are of a jammy consistency. Remove from the heat and set aside or seal and store following the instructions on page 62.

To make the Blue Cheese Dressing, put the sour/soured cream, buttermilk, lemon juice, dill, salt and pepper in a mixing bowl and mix well. Add the crumbled Stilton, stir through and set aside.

Rub the steaks with olive oil and season with salt and pepper.

Place a ridged griddle/grill pan over a high heat and get it really hot before placing the steaks into it. Cook for about 3 minutes on each side, then place on a plate and cover with foil to allow the meat to rest.

Lightly toast the sourdough bread and spread a generous layer of Beetroot/Beet Jam/Jelly on the bottom of four of the slices. Put the watercress over the Beetroot/Beet Jam/Jelly, and top with some sliced tomato.

Slice the rested steaks on the diagonal into 1-cm/½-inch slices and arrange over the tomato.

Spoon some Blue Cheese Dressing on top of the warm steak so that the cheese starts to melt and place the other slices of toasted bread on top. Serve.

FISH FINGER BAPS WITH PLUM KETCHUP MAYO, CUCUMBER & RADISH PICKLE & BABY GEM LETTUCE

2 x 280 g/10 oz. firm white fish
   fillets, such as cod, haddock,
   pollock or hake
3 tablespoons plain/all-purpose
   flour
¼ teaspoon ground white pepper
½ teaspoon sea salt
1 egg, lightly beaten
40 g/1 cup panko breadcrumbs
½ teaspoon dried chilli/hot
   red pepper flakes
1 tablespoon freshly chopped
   flat-leaf parsley
1 tablespoon finely grated
   Parmesan cheese
vegetable oil or sunflower oil,
   for frying
2 tablespoons Plum Ketchup
   (see page 124)
2 tablespoons mayonnaise
2 brioche burger buns,
   halved and lightly toasted
1 Little Gem/Bibb lettuce, leaves
   separated
Cucumber & Radish Pickle
   (see recipe below)
2 tablespoons coriander/
   cilantro leaves

CUCUMBER & RADISH PICKLE
75 ml/5 tablespoons rice wine
   vinegar
15 g/4 teaspoons sugar
¾ teaspoon sea salt
1 cucumber, thinly sliced into
   discs using a mandolin
4 radishes, thinly sliced into discs
   on a mandolin
½ teaspoon black sesame seeds

SERVES 2

We all feel nostalgic for this comfort food classic. Our Asian twist on this humble sandwich transforms it into something quite sublime.

To make the Cucumber & Radish Pickle, combine the vinegar, sugar and salt with 2 tablespoons of water in a small saucepan and heat over a gentle heat until the sugar and salt have dissolved. Remove from the heat and add the cucumber, radishes and sesame seeds. Stir and transfer to a sealable container and set aside. This will keep in the fridge for up to 1 week.

Preheat the oven to 180°C (350°F) Gas 4.

Cut the fish fillets into fingers. Depending on the size of the fillet, you should get about four per fillet – approximately 3 x 8 cm/1¼ x 3¼ inches each.

Take three shallow dishes. Mix the flour, white pepper and salt in one, pour the beaten egg into another, and combine the breadcrumbs, chilli/hot red pepper flakes, parsley and Parmesan in the third.

Using one hand to do each step, coat the fish fingers, one by one, in the seasoned flour, then in the egg wash, shaking off any excess, and then roll in the breadcrumbs to coat. Transfer to a clean plate.

Pour 1 cm/½ inch of oil into a large frying pan/skillet and heat. To check if the oil is hot enough, put a breadcrumb into the pan and if it sizzles, it is ready. Cook the fish fingers in the hot oil until lightly brown, then turn over and brown the other side. Transfer to a lined baking sheet and place in the preheated oven for 3 minutes.

In a small bowl, combine the Plum Ketchup with the mayonnaise and mix together. Set aside.

To assemble, put a generous spoonful of the plum ketchup mayonnaise on the top and bottom of each toasted brioche bun. Place two lettuce leaves on each bun, then the fish fingers, and top with some Cucumber & Radish Pickle, coriander/cilantro leaves and the top of the bun. Serve.

PRODUCE & INGREDIENTS

It staggers me when I hear statistics on the amount of food the average household throws out. My parents instilled in me an aversion to food wastage. When I was growing up, Sunday night presented a prime opportunity to transform the week's leftovers into dinner. As you can imagine this 'clearing out the fridge' approach to cooking had mixed results, but on the whole, they were tasty and satisfying dishes. Leftover meat became a curry, any combination of cooked vegetables were smothered in white sauce or breadcrumbs and baked, and there were endless risottos and pasta sauces.

While I don't think it was intentional, my parents' approach to cooking shaped the way I think about ingredients and recipes. It is all well and good to encourage people to eat seasonally and to buy local and organic ingredients. Equally as important is how resourceful we can be with the ingredients we have, to avoid wasting food or throwing food away because it has been forgotten about and left in the fridge to spoil.

It requires a spirit of adventure, but I'd encourage you to treat recipes as a guide rather than a rigid set of instructions. Substitute ingredients with what you already have or what you can see is in season when you go shopping. Not only will you create new dishes and discover new flavour combinations, you will save money by not throwing food out and get better flavour (and value) from seasonal ingredients grown locally.

I always try to build a meal from something left over from the previous night. Over the course of a week, elements of meals become intertwined and leftovers provide inspiration for the next night's dinner. Leftover roast vegetables become bubble and squeak, leftover caponata becomes a pasta sauce, leftover baked chicken is shredded for a chicken noodle salad, or leftover wild mushroom stew, topped with puff pastry, is transformed into a pot pie. This approach to using leftovers extends to the cafés as well. One of our most popular dishes was a 'rib-wich', created one day when we had an abundance of sticky Asian pork ribs from the dinner menu. The chef shredded the meat, crisped it on the grill and served it in a toasted ciabatta with hot sauce and aioli for lunch.

Our motto: resourcefulness is the mother of deliciousness.

SHAVED FENNEL SALAD
WITH WALNUTS, PARMESAN & POMEGRANATE

If I had to choose a desert island luxury item it would be a mandolin as it is one of my most prized and well used tools in the kitchen. Using a mandolin to slice vegetables will transform your salads – courgettes/zucchini, beetroot/beets, fennel and carrots are all delicious raw when thinly sliced and dressed simply with lemon juice and olive oil.

4 tablespoons olive oil, plus extra to serve
grated zest of 1 lemon
3 tablespoons freshly squeezed lemon juice
15 g/¼ cup chopped chives
½ teaspoon sea salt
600 g/1¼ lbs. (about 2 medium) fennel bulbs, trimmed and thinly sliced
1 pear, cored, quartered and thinly sliced
seeds of 1 pomegranate
60 g/⅔ cup walnuts, toasted
60 g/1 cup Parmesan shavings
70 g/1¼ cups rocket/arugula
freshly ground black pepper

SERVES 6

Begin by whisking the oil together with the lemon zest and juice in a large mixing bowl. Add the chives, salt and some pepper to taste.

Add the sliced fennel and pear, and gently toss in the dressing to prevent any discolouration.

Add the remaining ingredients, one at a time, and gently mix together.

Serve with an extra drizzle of olive oil.

MUSHROOM, PEAS & SPINACH WITH HERB PESTO

3 tablespoons olive oil
1 garlic clove, sliced
8 Portobello or large flat mushrooms
350 g/3 cups frozen peas, defrosted
80 g/1½ cups baby spinach
3 tablespoons pine nuts/kernels, toasted

HERB PESTO
20 g/scant ¼ cup pine nuts/kernels
10 g/scant ¼ cup basil leaves
20 g/1 cup mint leaves
½ garlic clove, grated
½ teaspoon grated lemon zest
1 tablespoon freshly squeezed lemon juice
25 g/⅓ cup grated Parmesan cheese
3 tablespoons olive oil
½ teaspoon sea salt
freshly ground black pepper

SERVES 4–6

Preheat the oven to 180°C (350°F) Gas 4.

To prepare the mushrooms, heat the oil in a small saucepan or pot set over a medium heat. Add the sliced garlic and cook gently for 2 minutes. Arrange the whole mushrooms, stalk-side up, on a baking sheet. Spoon the oil and cooked garlic over the mushrooms, cover with foil and cook in the preheated oven for 10 minutes. Remove the foil and cook for another 15–20 minutes, or until the mushrooms are tender. Remove from the oven and set aside to cool.

To make the Herb Pesto, place all of the ingredients in a food processor and blend.

Slice the baked mushrooms into 5-mm/¼-inch pieces and put in a large mixing bowl with the defrosted peas and Herb Pesto. Add the baby spinach and toss everything together. Sprinkle the toasted pine nuts/kernels on top and serve.

QUINOA & RED RICE SALAD
WITH CASHEW NUTS & CITRUS GINGER DRESSING

Quinoa is one of those slightly tricky grains that can be bland and soggy if under-seasoned and overcooked. I find that toasting the quinoa before boiling it in water gives it a lovely nutty flavour and helps it retain its texture.

2 red onions, peeled and cut into wedges, root intact
3 tablespoons olive oil
1 teaspoon soft light brown sugar
60 g/^{2}/$_3$ cup cashew nuts
200 g/1^1/$_4$ cups quinoa
200 g/1 cup Camargue red rice
100 g/^{2}/$_3$ cup (dark) raisins
2 handfuls of rocket/arugula
4 spring onions/scallions, thinly sliced
sea salt and freshly ground black pepper

CITRUS GINGER DRESSING
75 ml/5 tablespoons olive oil
1 tablespoon sesame oil
grated zest and freshly squeezed juice of 1 orange
1 tablespoon rice wine vinegar
a 5-cm/2-inch piece of fresh ginger, peeled and finely grated
1 long red chilli/chile, deseeded and finely diced
1 garlic clove, finely grated

SERVES 6

Preheat the oven to 170°C (325°F) Gas 3.

Put the onion wedges on a baking sheet and drizzle with the olive oil, sprinkle with the brown sugar and season with salt and pepper. Roast in the preheated oven for 25 minutes, until meltingly soft. Remove from the oven and set aside to cool completely.

Meanwhile, scatter the cashew nuts on a separate baking sheet and toast in the oven for 8 minutes. Remove from the oven and set aside to cool.

Once you have toasted the cashew nuts, spread the quinoa evenly on another baking sheet and toast in the oven for 10 minutes.

Set two saucepans or pots filled with salted water over a medium heat and bring to the boil. Add the red rice to one pan and |simmer for 20 minutes. Add the toasted quinoa to the other pan and simmer for 9 minutes. Once cooked, both should still have a little bite.

Drain off the water in both pans using a fine mesh sieve/strainer. Transfer the quinoa and rice to a large mixing bowl and set aside to cool.

To make the Citrus Ginger Dressing, mix all the ingredients together in a small bowl, using a whisk to emulsify the oils with the orange juice and vinegar.

Pour the dressing into the bowl with the rice and quinoa. Add the roasted red onions, toasted cashew nuts, (dark) raisins, rocket/arugula and spring onions/scallions. Season with salt and pepper and serve.

GREEN BEAN & TOASTED CORN SALAD WITH MISO

2 tablespoons
vegetable oil
2 cobs of corn, peeled
300 g/2¼ cups green
beans, ends trimmed
2 baby gem lettuces,
washed and cut into
3-cm/1¼-inch rounds
25 g/½ cup coriander/
cilantro, roughly
chopped
½ long red chilli/chile,
deseeded and cut
into thin rounds
1 tablespoon sesame
seeds, toasted

MISO DRESSING
1½ tablespoons white
miso paste
3 tablespoons
vegetable oil
2 teaspoons sesame oil
1 tablespoon rice wine
vinegar
1½ tablespoons mirin
or 1 tablespoon
granulated sugar
1 teaspoon grated
lemon zest
1 tablespoon freshly
squeezed lemon juice
1 garlic clove, crushed
¼ teaspoon sea salt

SERVES 2–4

Heat the oil in a frying pan/skillet set over a medium heat and add the corn. Cook for 8–10 minutes, turning occasionally until lightly charred in parts and tender. Remove from the pan and set aside to cool. When the corn is cool enough to handle, stand it on its end on a chopping board and run a sharp knife down the sides to remove the corn kernels from the cores. Transfer the corn to a large mixing bowl and discard the cores.

Set a large saucepan of salted water over a medium-high heat and bring to the boil. Blanch the beans for 2–3 minutes, drain and cool. Add the beans, lettuce, coriander/cilantro and chilli/chile to the corn and gently toss together. For the Miso Dressing, place all the ingredients in a clean, screw top jar; shake to combine. Add enough dressing to coat the vegetables and toss together. Sprinkle with toasted sesame seeds. Serve.

KOHLRABI & SPROUT SLAW WITH HAZELNUTS

500 g/5 cups Brussels
sprouts, thinly sliced
500 g/18 oz. kohlrabi,
peeled, quartered
and thinly sliced
100 g/¾ cup (about
2 stalks) celery, thinly
sliced on the diagonal
150 g/1½ cups (about
1 medium) green
apple, peeled, cored
and thinly sliced
20 g/scant ½ cup mint,
roughly chopped
20 g/scant ½ cup
chervil, roughly
chopped
80 g/¾ cup roasted and
skinned hazelnuts,
chopped

DRESSING
1 teaspoon English
mustard
60 ml/¼ cup apple cider
vinegar
125 ml/½ cup extra
virgin olive oil
2 tablespoons maple
syrup
2 tablespoons crème
fraîche
1 tablespoon poppy
seeds
sea salt and freshly
ground black pepper

SERVES 2–4

This slaw is really easy to make. Place all the slaw ingredients in a large mixing bowl and toss to combine.

To make the dressing, put all the ingredients into a small bowl and whisk to combine. Adjust the seasoning to taste.

Add the dressing to the slaw and toss to coat all the ingredients before serving.

ORZO WITH ROAST COURGETTES & SEMI-DRIED TOMATO DRESSING

If the thought of pasta salad makes you recoil with images of cold pasta mixed with canned corn, drowned in mayo, fear not – this fresh, vibrant salad bears no resemblance.

250 g/4 cups orzo pasta
400 g/12 oz. (about 2) courgettes/
    zucchinis, cut in half lengthways
70 g/²/₃ cup feta cheese
70 g/²/₃ cup black olives, pitted
    and halved
20 g/scant ¹/₂ cup flat-leaf parsley,
    chopped

DRESSING
1 bulb garlic
125 ml/¹/₂ cup olive oil,
    plus 2 teaspoons to roast,
    and extra to serve
80 g/³/₄ cup semi-dried tomatoes
    in oil, drained
¹/₄ teaspoon caster/granulated
    sugar
1 tablespoon balsamic vinegar
sea salt and freshly ground
    black pepper

SERVES 6

Preheat the oven to 200°C (400°F) Gas 6.

Begin by making the dressing. Cut the top off the garlic bulb to expose the individual garlic cloves. Place the garlic bulb, cut-side down, onto a square piece of foil and drizzle with 2 teaspoons of olive oil. Lift the foil up around the garlic and place on a baking sheet. Roast in the preheated oven for 45 minutes. Remove from the oven, open the foil wrap and set aside to cool. When the garlic is cool enough to handle, squeeze the cloves out of the skin, coarsely chop the garlic flesh and discard the skin.

Reduce the oven temperature to 180°C (350°F) Gas 4.

Place 50 g/¹/₂ cup of the semi-dried tomatoes in a food processor with the remaining olive oil, the sugar, vinegar, and some salt and pepper. Blend and pour into a large mixing bowl.

Roughly chop the remaining semi-dried tomatoes and stir through the blended mixture with the roasted garlic.

To prepare the orzo pasta, add it to a saucepan or pot of salted boiling water set over a medium heat. Bring to the boil and cook for about 8 minutes until al dente. Drain well before transferring to the bowl of dressing while still warm. Toss to coat the orzo.

Preheat a grill-pan over a medium heat and, when hot, grill the courgettes/zucchinis, flesh-side down for 2 minutes until marked. Transfer the courgettes/zucchinis skin-side down to a baking sheet, season with salt and pepper and cook in the still-warm oven for 10 minutes. Remove from the oven and cut on the diagonal at 2-cm/³/₄-inch intervals.

Add the courgettes/zucchinis, feta, olives and parsley to the orzo mixture and stir. Add a final drizzle of olive oil and serve.

CRUNCHY BULGUR SALAD

This is a salad of contrasts. Sweet and bitter, soft and crunchy, and a rainbow of autumnal colours. Hearty enough as brunch on its own.

250 g/1 1/2 cups medium or coarse bulgur wheat
200 g/7 oz. (about 1 small) fennel bulb, trimmed and thinly sliced
grated zest and freshly squeezed juice of 1/2 lemon
200 g/1 1/2 cups (about 4 stalks) celery, thinly sliced on the diagonal
100 g/3/4 cup dried pitted dates, roughly chopped
1/2 small radicchio, cored and leaves finely shredded
75 g/3/4 cup walnuts, roughly chopped
20 g/scant 1/2 cup flat-leaf parsley, roughly chopped
20 g/scant 1/2 cup mint, roughly chopped
sea salt and freshly ground black pepper

DRESSING
1 garlic clove, peeled
1 teaspoon sea salt
2 teaspoons pomegranate molasses
50 ml/3 1/2 tablespoons olive oil
1 teaspoon ground cinnamon

SERVES 6

Begin by making the dressing. Crush the garlic to a paste with the salt using a pestle and mortar. Transfer to a small mixing bowl and whisk together with all the remaining ingredients. Cover and set aside.

Put the bulgur wheat into a separate large mixing bowl. Add just enough boiling water to wet the grains but not go above the surface. Cover with clingfilm/plastic wrap and set aside for 15–20 minutes, until just tender but still with a bit of bite. Drain off any excess moisture using a fine mesh sieve/strainer, if necessary.

Place the sliced fennel in another large mixing bowl and dress immediately with the lemon zest and juice to prevent any discolouration. Add all the remaining ingredients and the soaked bulgur wheat.

Pour over the prepared dressing and season with extra salt and pepper, to taste. Serve on a large plate with salad servers.

SUPERFOOD BOWL WITH SMOKED SALMON, QUINOA, AVOCADO & CASHEW TURMERIC YOGURT DRESSING

You can make this bowl vegetarian by using grilled halloumi instead of the smoked salmon. It is also gluten-free.

300 g/10½ oz. curly kale
2 teaspoons tamari
2 teaspoons apple cider vinegar
4 tablespoons plus 2 teaspoons olive oil
200 g/1 cup quinoa
1 head of broccoli (approx. 350 g/12 oz.) cut into long bite-sized florets
seeds from ½ pomegranate
1 long red chilli/chile, deseeded and thinly sliced
15 g/½ oz. dill, roughly chopped
grated zest of ½ lemon
2 tablespoons freshly squeezed lemon juice
2 ripe avocados
200 g/1 cup sliced smoked salmon
15 g/2 tablespoons pumpkin seeds, toasted
sea salt and freshly ground black pepper

CASHEW TURMERIC YOGURT DRESSING

140 g/1 generous cup raw unsalted cashew nuts
1 tablespoon maple syrup
300 g/1½ cups Greek yogurt
1 teaspoon apple cider vinegar
½ teaspoon sea salt
1 teaspoon ground turmeric
1 teaspoon olive oil

SERVES 4

To make the Cashew Turmeric Yogurt Dressing, put the cashew nuts in a small bowl and cover with water. Allow the nuts to soak in room temperature water for a couple of hours, or overnight. Drain the cashews and blitz in a blender with the other ingredients. The dressing will keep in the fridge in a sealed container for up to 1 week and is delicious served with any salad or vegetables.

To make the salad, pull the kale from its central stalks and tear the leaves into small pieces. Put the kale in a bowl and add the tamari, apple cider vinegar and 2 teaspoons of olive oil. Scrunch it in your hands for a minute to coat the leaves and soften them a little.

Rinse the quinoa and place in a saucepan with double the volume of salted water and bring to the boil. Reduce the heat and simmer gently for 12 minutes until cooked. Drain into a colander and cool.

Bring a separate saucepan of salted water to the boil. Add the broccoli florets and simmer for a couple of minutes, then drain and run under cold water so the broccoli stays crunchy and does not continue to cook.

In a large bowl, combine the cooked quinoa, kale, broccoli, pomegranate seeds, chilli/chile and dill.

Make a lemon dressing by putting the lemon zest, lemon juice, 4 tablespoons olive oil and salt and pepper in a small screw-top jar. Shake and then pour over the quinoa salad mix and toss together.

Cut the avocados in half, pit then remove the flesh and slice.

Distribute the quinoa salad between four bowls. Arrange the avocado and smoked salmon slices over the top of the salad in each bowl, then drizzle with the Cashew Turmeric Yogurt Dressing. Finally, sprinkle with the toasted pumpkin seeds. Serve.

GRILLED HALLOUMI
WITH ROAST SHALLOTS, BEETROOT & VINCOTTO

Vincotto is a naturally sweet 'cooked wine' syrup that can be used in both sweet and savoury dishes. It pairs beautifully with the salty halloumi cheese and earthy beetroot/beet in this salad. If you can't find vincotto, you can substitute balsamic vinegar with a little honey. Like wine, vincottos vary a lot in quality so buy the best that you can find.

50 g/½ cup pecans, toasted, chopped
25 g/½ cup flat-leaf parsley, chopped
2 tablespoons olive oil
250 g/9 oz. halloumi, cut into
   1-cm/½-inch slices
freshly squeezed juice of ½ a lemon

ROAST BEETROOT/BEETS
750 g/1 lb. 10 oz. (about 4 medium)
   beetroots/beets
2 tablespoons olive oil
1 tablespoon vincotto (or 1
   tablespoon each of balsamic
   vinegar and clear honey)
1 teaspoon fennel seeds
sea salt and freshly ground
   black pepper

ROAST SHALLOTS
300 g/2 cups peeled and quartered
   shallots
1 tablespoon olive oil
½ tablespoon vincotto (or
   ½ tablespoon each of balsamic
   vinegar and clear honey)

VINCOTTO DRESSING
2 teaspoons vincotto
   (or 2 teaspoons each of balsamic
   vinegar and clear honey)
2 tablespoons olive oil
1 teaspoon clear honey
1 garlic clove, crushed

SERVES 2

Begin by preparing the Roast Beetroot/Beets. Put them in a saucepan or pot of boiling water and cook for about 40 minutes, until just tender. Drain and set aside to cool.

Once cool enough to handle, peel and cut into wedges.

Preheat the oven to 180°C (350°F) Gas 4.

Place the beetroot/beet wedges in a large mixing bowl with the oil, vincotto (or substitute) and fennel seeds. Toss to ensure everything is well coated, then spread out on a baking sheet. Season with salt and pepper and roast in the preheated oven for 30 minutes.

Meanwhile, prepare the Roast Shallots. Place them in a large mixing bowl with the oil and vincotto (or substitute). Toss together and spread out on a baking sheet. Season and roast in the oven for about 15 minutes, until soft.

To make the Vincotto Dressing, place the vincotto, oil, honey and crushed garlic in a clean screw-top jar. Close the jar and shake. Season with salt and pepper.

Place the Roast Beetroot/Beets, Roast Shallots, pecans and parsley in a large mixing bowl and gently toss together with the Vincotto Dressing and set aside until ready to serve.

Heat the olive oil in a large frying pan/skillet and fry the halloumi slices for 2 minutes on each side, until golden brown. Remove from the pan and drain on paper towels.

Serve the vegetable salad in bowls with the halloumi arranged on top. Squeeze the lemon juice over the cheese and enjoy.

BREADS
& BAKES

300 g/4 cups (about 2) grated courgette/ zucchini

300 g/2²⁄₃ cups self-raising/ rising flour, sifted

1 teaspoon baking powder

1 teaspoon mustard powder

¹⁄₂ teaspoon sea salt

¹⁄₂ teaspoon cayenne pepper

170 g/1²⁄₃ cups grated strong/ sharp Cheddar cheese

100 g/6¹⁄₂ tablespoons butter, melted

4 eggs, beaten

135 ml/¹⁄₂ cup plus 1 tablespoon milk

a 900-g/2-lb. loaf pan, greased and lined with baking parchment

MAKES 8–10 SLICES AND SERVES 4

COURGETTE LOAF

This is a great alternative to savoury muffins in the morning. Its loaf shape makes it easy to toast – thick slices, lightly toasted under a grill/broiler, then spread with butter and Tomato Chilli Jam (page 124) beat savoury muffins hands down.

Preheat the oven to 180°C (350°F) Gas 4.

Squeeze the grated courgette/zucchini with your hands to get rid of as much moisture as possible and place in a large mixing bowl with the flour, baking powder, mustard powder, salt, cayenne pepper and grated Cheddar. Toss everything together gently with your hands.

Combine the melted butter with the beaten eggs and milk in a jug/pitcher. Pour over the courgette/zucchini mixture and gently combine using a large spoon. Take care not to overwork the mixture – you should have a thick batter.

Spoon the mixture into the prepared loaf pan and bake in the preheated oven for 50 minutes–1 hour, until golden brown and a skewer inserted into the middle comes out clean.

Set aside to cool in the pan for 5 minutes, then turn out onto a wire rack to cool completely.

Slice, toast and butter the courgette/zucchini loaf to serve.

CHERRY TOMATO, ROSEMARY, CHEDDAR & GOAT'S CHEESE MUFFINS

These are perfect for an 'elevenses' treat when it's not quite lunchtime but you feel like a little smackerel of something. Some Tomato Chilli Jam (see page 124) or chutney dolloped on top of the muffins before they go into the oven is not essential but gives them a delicious sticky topping.

235 ml/scant 1 cup milk
60 ml/¼ cup olive oil
1 egg
250 g/2 cups plain/all-purpose flour
1 tablespoon baking powder
80 g/1 cup Cheddar cheese, grated
1 sprig of rosemary, leaves picked and finely chopped
½ teaspoon table salt
a pinch of ground white pepper
90 g/½ cup cherry tomatoes
50 g/⅓ cup goat's cheese
Tomato Chilli Jam or chutney (see page 124) (optional)

a 6-hole muffin pan, greased and lined with baking parchment squares

MAKES 6 MUFFINS

Preheat the oven to 170°C (325°F) Gas 3.

Whisk the milk, oil and egg together in a bowl. In a separate bowl mix together the flour, baking powder, grated Cheddar cheese, rosemary, salt and pepper. Add the wet mix to the dry ingredients and carefully fold together with a large spoon or spatula until just combined.

Cut the cherry tomatoes in half crossways and gently fold into the batter.

Divide the batter between the six prepared muffin moulds. Divide the goat's cheese into six even pieces and put one in the centre of each muffin, gently pressing it into the centre of the muffin batter. Finally, put about a teaspoon of Tomato Chilli Jam or chutney (if using) on top of each.

Bake in the preheated oven for 25 minutes, or until risen and golden brown. Remove from the pan and eat while still warm.

CHEDDAR CORNBREAD

Like the Courgette Loaf on page 98, this is more of a savoury cake than bread. Cut it into thick slices, butter each side and griddle or fry in a frying pan/skillet to get it nice and golden brown. Spread with Tomato Chilli Jam (see page 124) for a sweet and spicy kick.

75 g/5 tablespoons melted butter, plus extra for greasing
250 ml/1 cup buttermilk
170 ml/¾ cup milk
1 egg, lightly beaten
170 g/1⅓ cups quick-cook polenta/cornmeal
120 g/1¼ cups grated strong/sharp Cheddar cheese
3 Bird's eye chillies/chiles, deseeded and finely chopped
2 teaspoons salt
2 tablespoons freshly chopped chives
250 g/2 cups plain/all-purpose flour, sifted
2½ teaspoons baking powder
butter, to serve
Tomato Chilli Jam, to serve (see page 124)

a 900-g/2-lb. loaf pan, greased and lined with baking parchment

MAKES 8 SLICES AND SERVES 4

Preheat the oven to 180°C (350°F) Gas 4.

Put the melted butter, buttermilk, milk, beaten egg and polenta/cornmeal into a large mixing bowl, stir to mix and set aside for 10 minutes.

Fold in the grated Cheddar, Bird's eye chillies/chiles, salt and chopped chives.

Sift in the flour and baking powder and fold until just combined, taking care not to overmix.

Pour into the prepared loaf pan and bake in the preheated oven for 30–35 minutes, until golden brown and a skewer inserted into the middle comes out clean.

Set aside to cool in the pan for 5 minutes, then turn out onto a wire rack to cool completely.

Slice, toast and butter the cornbread, and serve with Tomato Chilli Jam.

FOCACCIA WITH THYME & NIGELLA SEEDS

One of the foods I miss most from Australia is the fantastic Turkish flatbread or pide that makes an appearance as 'toast' on many brunch menus. Focaccia has a similar spongy texture and makes an impressive centrepiece for a brunch feast. It's a great base for all sorts of flavours and for mopping up sauces or eggs.

1½ teaspoons active dried yeast granules
1 teaspoon caster/granulated sugar
310 g/11 oz. lukewarm water
500 g/3½ –3⅔ cups strong white/bread flour
1½ teaspoons table salt
50 ml/3½ tablespoons olive oil, plus extra for kneading and finishing
6 large pitted green or black olives, halved
1 teaspoon sea salt
½ bunch of thyme
½ teaspoon nigella seeds

30 x 40-cm/12 x 16-inch baking sheet lined with baking parchment, greased lightly with oil

MAKES 1 AND SERVES 8–10

In a jug/pitcher, mix the yeast and sugar with the lukewarm water and set aside for 5 minutes.

Mix the flour and table salt together in a large bowl. Add the oil to the water mixture and pour the wet mixture into the dry ingredients in the bowl and gently stir with your hand to form a dough.

Knead the dough in the bowl until it is holding together, then tip the dough out onto a lightly oiled surface and continue kneading for another 5 minutes until it starts to form a soft, smooth skin. When the dough feels soft and elastic, transfer it to a clean bowl, greased with some oil. Brush the top of the dough with oil and cover the bowl with a clean kitchen towel.

Set aside in a warm place and leave to rise for approximately 1 hour until doubled in size.

Tip the dough onto the prepared baking sheet and stretch out to cover the base of the sheet. Cover with clingfilm/plastic wrap and leave to rise again in a warm place for 45 minutes.

Preheat the oven to 210°C (400°F) Gas 6.

Use your fingers to make deep dimples in the focaccia at regular intervals. Push the halved olives into the dimples, drizzle the focaccia with olive oil and sprinkle with the sea salt, sprigs of thyme and the nigella seeds.

Bake in the preheated oven for 20 minutes, until it is golden and the base sounds hollow when you tap it. Remove the focaccia from the baking sheet, take off the parchment paper and allow the bread to cool on a wire rack.

This will taste delicious fresh from the oven but will also keep well (wrapped) for a couple of days and can be sliced and toasted.

BANANA BREAD WITH RASPBERRY LABNE

Banana bread is absolutely delicious on its own or toasted with butter, but if you want an indulgent start to the day, try it with this beautiful Raspberry Labne. Labne is a strained yogurt which has a consistency somewhere between cream cheese and yogurt. The longer you leave it, the firmer it becomes, so play around with the consistency.

125 g/1 stick unsalted butter, softened
250 g/1¼ cups caster/granulated sugar
2 large eggs, beaten
1 teaspoon pure vanilla extract
250 g/2 cups plain/all-purpose flour
2 teaspoons baking powder
4 very ripe bananas, peeled and mashed

RASPBERRY LABNE
150 g/1 generous cup fresh or frozen raspberries
100 g/½ cup caster/granulated sugar
500 g/2 cups Greek yogurt
1 teaspoon pure vanilla extract

a 900-g/2-lb. loaf pan, greased and lined with baking parchment
2 fine mesh sieves/strainers, 1 lined with several layers of muslin/cheesecloth

MAKES 8–10 SLICES AND SERVES 4

Preheat the oven to 180°C (350°F) Gas 4.

Beat the butter and caster/granulated sugar together in a large mixing bowl until light, fluffy and a pale cream colour. Gradually beat in the eggs, one at a time, before adding the vanilla.

In a separate bowl, sift together the flour and baking powder.

Gently fold the mashed bananas into the wet mixture, a little at a time, alternating with the sifted flour mixture so that the mixture doesn't split.

Transfer the banana batter to the prepared loaf pan, then bake in the preheated oven for 20 minutes.

Reduce the oven temperature to 160°C (325°F) Gas 3 and cook for a further 40–45 minutes until golden brown, firm to the touch and a skewer inserted into the middle comes out clean.

Set aside to cool in the pan for 5 minutes, then turn out onto a wire rack to cool completely.

To make the Raspberry Labne, place 50 g/½ cup of the raspberries in a small saucepan or pot with the sugar and 100 ml/scant ½ cup of water. Set over a gentle heat and simmer until it reduces by a-third.

Remove from the heat and strain through the unlined sieve/strainer set over a mixing bowl. Discard the raspberry pulp, cover the syrup and set aside to cool completely.

Add the yogurt, vanilla and remaining raspberries to the raspberry syrup and mix together. Pour the mixture into the lined sieve/strainer set over a mixing bowl. Draw the cloth together, twist the gathered cloth to form a tight ball and tie the ends with kitchen string. Suspend the wrapped labne over the bowl and put in the fridge for 12–24 hours. Discard the drained water and transfer the labne to a bowl, ready to serve with slices of banana bread.

CAFE CULTURE

'Once you find a café you love you go again and again because it makes the city feel smaller; to feel the warmth of people who recognize you, know your name and know what coffee you drink.'
ALBERTO, LANTANA REGULAR

Not everyone is lucky enough to have a fantastic local café on their doorstep. Somewhere welcoming that smells of freshly ground coffee and delicious food being prepared, where the staff greet you by name, and the personality and passion of the owner is stamped on every lampshade, piece of crockery and each item on the menu.

When I first moved to London, I was struck by how few good independent cafés there were and instead, how corporate, homogenous chain cafés and coffee shops dominated the high street. Customers would bustle in and out, head down, absorbed in their own world, eager to get their coffee as quickly as possible and be on their way. This has changed dramatically in the last ten years, as more and more unique, quirky cafés have emerged – a testament to London's coffee house history.

In the 17th century after the Great Fire of London destroyed the Royal Exchange building, coffee houses became de facto trading houses and community hubs. People from all walks of life would sit at communal tables and talk, sharing ideas and engaging in political and intellectual debate. Coffee houses were an integral part of both working and social life.

I see this coffee house culture first-hand at our cafés with our eclectic customer base. Whether it's friends catching up, local workers holding meetings, freelancers with laptops sharing a table with other freelancers using the café as a temporary office space, couples enjoying a leisurely brunch together, people reading the newspaper in the sunshine, or strangers chatting to each other as they wait for a coffee to take away. There's a relaxed but vibrant community atmosphere and a sense that people are coming here for something more than just the food and coffee. When you find a good café it becomes an extension of your home and, in the words of one of our regulars, the city becomes a little smaller.

RASPBERRY & APPLE MUFFINS

Who doesn't love a freshly baked muffin, especially when they are bursting with fruit so you can convince yourself that they are healthy?

1 egg
180 g/1 scant cup golden caster/
    pure cane sugar
70 g/5 tablespoons unsalted
    butter, melted and cooled
180 ml/¾ cup milk
grated zest of 1 lemon
1 teaspoon pure vanilla extract
100 g/1 cup (about 1 small)
    peeled, cored and diced
    green apple
125g/1 generous cup fresh
    raspberries, plus 4 halved
    to decorate
270 g/2 cups plus 1 tablespoon
    self-raising/rising flour
½ teaspoon baking powder
¼ teaspoon sea salt
icing/confectioners' sugar, to dust

a 12-hole muffin pan lined with
    8 paper cases

MAKES 8 MUFFINS

Preheat the oven to 170°C (325°F) Gas 3.

Beat the egg and golden caster/pure cane sugar together in a large mixing bowl until light and a pale cream colour. Add the cooled melted butter, milk, lemon zest and vanilla, and mix until combined. Stir in the apple and raspberries, then sift in the flour, baking powder and salt. Gently fold the mixture with a large spoon – take care not to over beat the mixture and stop as soon as it comes together, even if it is still lumpy.

Divide the batter between the muffin cases and place a raspberry half on top of each.

Bake in the preheated oven for 30 minutes, until light brown and a skewer inserted into a muffin comes out clean.

Dust with icing/confectioners' sugar and serve straight from the oven. The muffins are best eaten on the day of baking but will keep for up to 2 days if stored in an airtight container.

BERRY FRIANDS

250 g/2 cups icing/confectioners'
  sugar
50 g/6 tablespoons plain/
  all-purpose flour
170 g/1¼ cups ground almonds
grated zest of 1 lemon
6 egg whites
200 g/1 stick plus 6 tablespoons
  unsalted butter, melted
85 g/⅔ cup blueberries
85 g/⅔ cup raspberries

*a 12-hole non-stick friand or
  mini muffin pan, well-greased*

MAKES 12 FRIANDS

When I moved to London, I discovered that the oval-shaped cake pans that are used to bake friands in Australia are virtually impossible to buy in the UK. Many a time have I returned to London from holidays in Australia with a heavy suitcase filled with cake pans. Friands will actually taste exactly the same if you make them in round mini muffin pans, but for me, a friand should always be oval.

Preheat the oven to 180°C (350°F) Gas 4.

Sift the icing/confectioners' sugar and flour into a large mixing bowl, then stir through the ground almonds and lemon zest.

In a separate bowl, lightly beat the egg whites with a whisk or fork to break them up, then stir them through the dry ingredients to make a smooth paste.

Add half of the melted butter to the batter and stir well before adding the remaining butter.

Fold in half of the blueberries and raspberries, then divide the batter evenly into the prepared pan – the holes should be two-thirds full.

Place the remaining berries on top and bake in the preheated oven for 15–20 minutes, until firm and golden brown.

Remove the pan from the oven and let it cool on a wire rack for about 10 minutes before turning the friands out.

Serve hot or cold – either way they're delicious!

LEMON POLENTA CAKES

There is always at least one gluten-free cake on the counter at the café and this is one of my favourites. I don't think the fact that it is flourless has anything to do with its popularity – it's just a delicious lemony treat.

200 g/1 stick plus 6 tablespoons butter, softened
230 g/1 cup plus 2½ tablespoons golden caster/raw cane sugar
3 eggs
200 g/1⅓ cups ground almonds
100 g/¾ cup polenta/cornmeal
1 teaspoon baking powder
3 lemons

LEMON ICING

1 tablespoon freshly squeezed lemon juice
250 g/2 cups icing/confectioners' sugar

8 x 170-ml/6-oz. pudding moulds, greased and base-lined with a small circle of baking parchment

MAKES 8

Preheat the oven to 170°C (325°F) Gas 3.

Beat the butter and 200 g/1 cup of the sugar together in a large mixing bowl, until light and fluffy. Add the eggs, one at a time, beating well after each addition. Add small amounts of ground almonds if the mixture begins to curdle. Add in the remaining ground almonds and beat well.

Stir in the polenta/cornmeal and baking powder. Add the grated zest and freshly squeezed juice of ½ lemon and stir again.

Divide the batter evenly between the prepared pudding moulds and put them on a baking sheet. Bake in the preheated oven for 20 minutes or until a skewer inserted into a cake comes out clean.

Meanwhile, make a lemon syrup. Place the grated zest and juice of the remaining lemons in a saucepan set over a gentle heat, with the remaining sugar. Stir to combine and heat until the sugar has dissolved completely.

Remove the cakes from the oven and prick all over with a skewer. Pour the lemon syrup over each cake and let it soak through – about 1 tablespoon per cake.

Leave to cool in the pudding moulds for 15 minutes before turning the cakes out to cool completely.

To make the Lemon Icing, add just enough lemon juice to the icing/confectioners' sugar for a thick but slightly runny consistency.

When ready to serve, spoon the lemon icing on top of the cakes and let it drip down their sides.

APPLE & BLACKBERRY STREUSEL CAKE

220 g/1¾ cups plain/
   all-purpose flour
½ teaspoon bicarbonate of/
   baking soda
1 teaspoon baking powder
a pinch of salt
85 g/6 tablespoons unsalted
   butter, softened
140 g/¾ cup granulated/
   white sugar
2 large eggs
1 teaspoon pure vanilla extract
200 ml/¾ cup sour/soured cream

APPLE FILLING
450 g/4½ cups peeled, cored and
   quartered Granny Smith apples
2 tablespoons caster/
   granulated sugar
150 g/1 generous cup fresh
   blackberries

STREUSEL TOPPING
80 g/⅓ cup light brown sugar
1 teaspoon ground cinnamon
a pinch of ground cloves
3 tablespoons granulated/
   white sugar
40 g/⅓ cup plain/all-purpose flour
a pinch of salt
40 g/3 tablespoons butter, cubed
20 g/2½ tablespoons chopped
   pecans

a 20-cm/8-inch round cake pan,
   greased and lined with baking
   parchment

SERVES 8–10

Part cake, part dessert; the complete package. Serve thick slices of this apple and blackberry cake with cream.

Begin by making the apple filling. Combine the quartered apples with the sugar and 3 tablespoons of water in a medium saucepan or pot. Set over a medium-high heat and bring to the boil. Reduce the heat, cover and simmer for about 5 minutes, until the apples are tender. Stir through the blackberries and set aside.

Next, prepare the streusel topping. Combine the light brown sugar, cinnamon and cloves in a medium mixing bowl. Stir in the granulated/white sugar, flour and salt. Add the cubed butter and rub into the mixture using your fingertips, until you have a crumbly texture. Stir in the pecans, cover and place in the freezer until ready to use.

Preheat the oven to 170°C (325°F) Gas 3.

Sift the flour, bicarbonate of/baking soda, baking powder and salt into a large mixing bowl.

In a separate bowl, cream the butter and sugar together until light and fluffy. Add the eggs and vanilla and beat until combined.

Add half of the flour mixture and half the sour/soured cream to the egg mixture and stir gently with a spatula until just combined. Repeat with the remaining flour and sour/soured cream.

Spread one-third of the mixture evenly over the base of the prepared cake pan. Top with the apple and blackberry filling. Spoon the remaining cake mixture on top and smooth over the surface with a palette knife.

Sprinkle the streusel topping evenly over the surface of the cake, and bake in the preheated oven for 55 minutes, until golden on top and a skewer inserted into the middle comes out clean, remembering that there will be some moisture from the fruit centre but the batter should be cooked through.

Remove from the oven and serve warm or cold, cut into slices.

ORANGE & HONEY CAKE

The honey-orange syrup on this cake helps to keep it lovely and moist, but it is still best eaten on the day it is made.

170 g/1 stick plus 4 tablespoons
   unsalted butter, softened
340 g/1¾ cups caster/
   granulated sugar
3 large eggs
2 teaspoons grated orange zest,
   plus extra to decorate
1½ teaspoons pure vanilla extract
300 ml/1¼ cups sour/soured
   cream
375 g/3 cups plain/all-purpose
   flour
2 teaspoons baking powder
½ teaspoon bicarbonate of/
   baking soda
a pinch of salt

SYRUP
100 g/scant ½ cup clear honey
100 ml/⅓ cup orange juice
1–2 tablespoons orange blossom
   water

TOPPING
85 g/6 tablespoons butter,
   softened
250 g/2 cups icing/confectioners'
   sugar
1 teaspoon pure vanilla extract
1 tablespoon clear honey

a 23-cm/9-inch round cake pan,
   greased and lined with baking
   parchment

SERVES 8

Preheat the oven to 170°C (325°F) Gas 3.

Cream the butter and caster/granulated sugar together in a large mixing bowl, until light and fluffy. Add the eggs, one at a time, then add the zest, vanilla and sour/soured cream.

In a separate bowl, sift the flour, baking powder, bicarbonate of/baking soda and salt. Gently fold into the butter mixture, until just combined.

Spoon the batter into the prepared cake pan and bake in the preheated oven for 50–60 minutes, or until the cake is springy to the touch and a skewer inserted into the middle comes out clean.

Meanwhile, make an orange syrup. Place the honey and orange juice in a saucepan or pot set over a gentle heat, with 150 ml/⅔ cup of water. Simmer for 5 minutes to reduce the syrup by half. Stir in the orange blossom water and remove from the heat.

Remove the cake from the oven and prick all over with a skewer. Pour over the orange syrup and let it soak through. Place on a wire rack to cool completely in the pan.

To make the topping, place the butter and icing/confectioners' sugar in a freestanding electric mixer and beat on a low speed, until combined. Increase the speed and beat for 3 minutes. Add the vanilla and honey and continue to beat for 1 minute, until smooth.

When the cake is completely cool, spread the topping over the cake and decorate with a little extra orange zest.

PRESERVES

One of the best reasons to make your own jam/jelly is that you can make it how you like it. A lot of jam/jelly recipes use equal amounts of sugar and fruit which I find too sweet, so I use half as much sugar – the jam/jelly is still sweet without obliterating the taste of the fruit.

APPLE & GINGER JAM

750 g/7$\frac{1}{2}$ cups (about 5 medium)
    green apples, peeled, cored
    and diced
grated zest and freshly squeezed
    juice of 1 lemon
375 g/scant 2 cups caster/
    granulated sugar
30 g/$\frac{1}{4}$ cup (2 balls) stem ginger,
    diced, plus 3 tablespoons syrup
1 teaspoon ground ginger
20 g/3 tablespoons peeled and
    finely grated fresh ginger

sterilized glass jars with airtight lids

MAKES 1 LITRE (35 FL OZ.)/ 4 CUPS

MIXED BERRY JAM
500 g/5 cups mixed
    fresh berries
250 g/2$\frac{1}{4}$ cups caster/
    granulated sugar
peeled zest of 1 lemon,
    cut into wide strips

MAKES 500 ML/2 CUPS

Place the apples and lemon zest and juice in a saucepan or pot set over a gentle heat and warm through until the apples are soft. Add the sugar, stem, ground and fresh gingers. Stir to combine and cook until the sugar has dissolved. It is important to dissolve the sugar before the jam/jelly reaches boiling point otherwise it may not set.

Increase the heat and bring the jam/jelly to the boil. Let it boil rapidly for 2 minutes then reduce the heat and simmer for 10 minutes, stirring occasionally, until the jam/jelly is thick. You should be able to run a spoon along the bottom of the pan and leave a path for a few seconds before the jam/jelly runs into it.

While still warm, spoon the jam/jelly into sterilized glass jars. Carefully tap them on the counter to get rid of any air pockets, wipe clean and tightly screw on the lids. Turn the jars upside down and leave until completely cold. Store unopened in a cool, dark place for up to 12 months. Once opened, store in the fridge and use within 2 weeks.

VARIATION To make Mixed Berry Jam, place all of the ingredients in a saucepan or pot set over a gentle heat, stir to combine, cook and store as above, removing the lemon peel before spooning the jam/jelly into jars.

TOMATO CHILLI JAM

Our chilli jam recipe has stood the test of time. On the menu since the day we opened, it has appeared as an accompaniment to a variety of dishes; sweet corn fritters, cheddar cornbread, burgers and halloumi.

1.5 kg/8 cups ripe tomatoes

6 garlic cloves, finely grated

6 red chillies/chiles, deseeded and finely chopped

400 ml/1²/₃ cups red wine vinegar

400 g/2 cups caster/ granulated sugar

sterilized, glass jars with airtight lids

MAKES 1 LITRE /4 CUPS

To peel the tomatoes, cut a cross in the base of each tomato and place in a large mixing bowl. Cover with boiling water and set aside for 5 minutes. The skin should then peel away easily. Discard the skin, roughly chop the flesh of the tomatoes and place in a medium saucepan or pot set over a medium heat.

Add all the remaining ingredients to the pan or pot and bring to the boil, then reduce the heat and simmer, uncovered, for about 2½–3 hours, stirring occasionally, until thick and glossy.

Remove the pan from the heat, and while still warm, spoon the jam/jelly into sterilized glass jars. Carefully tap them on the counter to get rid of any air pockets, wipe clean and tightly screw on the lids. Turn the jars upside down and leave until completely cold. Store unopened in a cool, dark place for up to 12 months. Once opened, store in the fridge and use within 2 weeks.

PLUM KETCHUP

The first time one of our new chefs tasted this ketchup she smiled, and said 'I could quite happily drink a bowl of that'. As with any ketchup it is an extremely versatile accompaniment, great with burgers of any kind or our Fish Finger Baps on page 79.

1 kg/6 cups (about 40) roughly chopped and pitted firm ripe plums

400 g/14 oz. onions, peeled and roughly chopped

2 Thai red chillies/ chiles, deseeded and roughly chopped

8 garlic cloves, roughly chopped

75 g/2³/₄ oz. ginger, peeled and grated

125 ml/¹/₂ cup soy sauce

500 ml/2 cups rice wine vinegar

3 star anise

¹/₄ teaspoon Chinese five-spice powder

250 g/1¹/₄ cups soft light brown sugar

sterilized, glass jars with airtight lids

MAKES 400 ML/ 1³/₄ CUPS

Put all the ingredients, except the sugar, into a lidded saucepan. Bring to the boil and then reduce the heat and simmer with the lid on until soft (approximately 30 minutes). Remove from the heat and leave overnight at room temperature for the flavours to develop.

The next day, push the mixture through a sieve/ strainer and retain the liquid. Discard the pulp, star anise and onion. Return the liquid to a clean pan, add the sugar and bring to the boil. Simmer gently, uncovered, for 2½ hours, stirring occasionally, until thick and glossy. While still hot, pour into a sterilized glass bottle or jar and seal with a lid. Store unopened in a cool, dark place for up to 12 months. Once opened, store in the fridge and use within 2 weeks.

PLUM CHUTNEY

1 kg/6 cups (about 40) roughly chopped and pitted firm ripe plums

1 kg/10 cups (about 7) peeled, cored and roughly chopped cooking apples

5 garlic cloves, chopped

300 g/2 cups (about 2) finely diced onions

475 ml/scant 2 cups cider vinegar

150 g/1 cup (dark) raisins

8 whole cloves

2$\frac{1}{2}$ teaspoons chilli/chili powder

2 large red chillies/chiles, deseeded and finely diced

125 ml/$\frac{1}{2}$ cup freshly squeezed lemon juice

$\frac{1}{2}$ tablespoon ground cumin

420 g/2 cups plus 1 tablespoon soft brown sugar

2 teaspoons sea salt

1 cinnamon stick, broken in half

2$\frac{1}{2}$ teaspoons peeled and grated fresh ginger

sterilized glass jars with airtight lids

MAKES 1.5 LITRES/6 CUPS

This punchy little chutney with plenty of kick makes an excellent accompaniment to a sausage sandwich or strong Cheddar cheese and crackers.

Place the plums, apples, garlic and onions in a saucepan or pot set over a gentle heat and slowly bring to the boil. Reduce the heat and simmer uncovered for 20–25 minutes, stirring occasionally.

Place the remaining ingredients in a large mixing bowl and stir well. Pour into the simmering plum mixture and stir using a wooden spoon. Continue to simmer uncovered for 1–1$\frac{1}{4}$ hours, stirring occasionally, until the mixture is thick and glossy.

Remove the pan from the heat, discard the cinnamon and while still warm, spoon the chutney into sterilized glass jars. Carefully tap them on the counter to get rid of any air pockets, wipe clean and tightly screw on the lids. Turn the jars upside down and leave until completely cold. Store unopened in a cool, dark place for up to 12 months. Once opened, store in the fridge and use within 2 weeks.

PEAR & APPLE CHUTNEY

This Pear & Apple Chutney is incredibly versatile and can elevate an otherwise simple dish into the perfect brunch-time treat.

100 ml/$\frac{1}{3}$ cup **vegetable oil**
230 g/1$\frac{1}{2}$ cups (about 2 small)
   finely diced red onions
1 kg/10 cups (about 7) **Braeburn**
   apples, finely diced
1 kg/4 cups (about 7) **pears,**
   peeled and finely diced
250 g/1$\frac{1}{4}$ cups **soft brown sugar**
250 g/1$\frac{1}{4}$ cups **dark brown sugar**
200 ml/$\frac{3}{4}$ cup **red wine vinegar**
2 tablespoons **ground ginger**
1 tablespoon **ground coriander**
1 tablespoon **ground allspice**

sterilized glass jars with
   airtight lids

MAKES 1.5 LITRES/6 CUPS

Heat the oil in a heavy-bottomed saucepan or pot set over a low heat. Sauté the onions, apples and pears until the onions are translucent. Add all the remaining ingredients and simmer uncovered for approximately 30 minutes, stirring occasionally, gently until the fruit is soft and the liquid has evaporated.

While still warm, spoon the chutney into sterilized glass jars. Carefully tap them on the counter to get rid of any air pockets, wipe clean and tightly screw on the lids. Store unopened in a cool, dark place for up to 12 months. Once opened, store in the fridge and use within 2 weeks.

DRINKS

POUR-OVER COFFEE

It is virtually impossible to make an espresso coffee at home that is as good as one made in a café by a trained barista using expensive commercial machinery. But if you want a hassle-free, inexpensive method for making delicious coffee at home, my advice is to make a filter coffee instead. Filter coffee is a longer, less intense drink than an espresso. By pouring the water slowly over coffee by hand, you can extract more of the delicate flavours and get to taste the characteristics of the coffee. Lighter roasted, single origin coffee is ideal for this method of coffee brewing.

17–18 g/¼ cup coffee beans
250–280 ml/1–1¼ cups boiling water

EQUIPMENT
a coffee grinder
a pouring kettle or jug/pitcher
a single-cup drip coffee cone
  and filter paper
a watch or timer

SERVES 1

It's always best to use freshly ground coffee, so it is worth investing in a small domestic grinder for home. Hand grinders are perfect if you are just making one or two cups. Grind your coffee beans on a medium grind for a paper filter.

Next, measure out your boiled water. You don't want to use the water as soon as it boils as this will burn the coffee. Pour 250 ml/1 cup into a pouring kettle or jug/pitcher while you're getting everything else ready, as this will allow the temperature to drop slightly.

Line your single-cup drip coffee cone with the paper filter and rinse it with hot water from the tap. This helps to get rid of the paper taste and allows the coffee to filter through more easily.

Put the ground coffee in the moistened filter and place it on top of your cup. Pour in enough boiled and slightly cooled water from your pouring kettle to saturate the grinds – the coffee will bloom and bubble. Over the next 3 minutes, very slowly pour the remaining water over the coffee. Pour in a circular motion to get an even distribution.

After 3 minutes you should have used up nearly all of the water in your pouring kettle, the water will have filtered through the ground coffee and your Pour-over Coffee is ready!

CHAI LATTE

1 teaspoon cardamom pods
1 teaspoon black peppercorns
1 teaspoon fennel seeds
1 teaspoon whole cloves
4 allspice berries
2 star anise
1 cinnamon stick
1 teaspoon ground ginger
2-cm/³⁄₄-inch piece of fresh
  ginger, peeled and sliced
150 g/³⁄₄ cup caster/
  granulated sugar
30 g/¹⁄₃ cup loose leaf black
  tea, such as Assam or
  English Breakfast
milk and ground cinnamon,
  to serve

SERVES 15

To make the syrup, put 1.5 litres/6 cups of water in a saucepan. Bruise the cardamom pods using a pestle and mortar and add to the saucepan with the other spices and fresh ginger. Bring to the boil, then reduce the heat and simmer for 10 minutes. Remove from the heat, add the sugar and tea, stir and leave to cool overnight. Strain into a clean empty milk container, put the lid on and store in the fridge.

To serve, pour 90 ml/¹⁄₃ cup of the syrup and 250 ml/1 cup of milk per person into a saucepan and heat gently. Pour into a mug and sprinkle with ground cinnamon.

COFFEE CULTURE

Coffee is to Australians what bread is to the French. It is an integral part of daily life and most people can't function without their morning hit. It might seem an unlikely passion for a nation associated with warm weather and cold beer, but Australians are proudly snobbish about their coffee and won't suffer a bad one lightly.

Cafés live and die by their coffee reputation. Customers will vote with their feet (and mouths) if a café doesn't source good beans, have skilled baristas and use proper coffee machines and equipment. It's not unusual for cafés to roast their own coffee or produce their own unique blend, as well as offer a number of different brew methods – pour-over, syphon, aeropress and of course, old school espresso.

Italian immigrants played a significant role in shaping Australia's coffee culture, bringing espresso coffee to its shores in the 1950s. For whatever reason, the expectation for good-quality espresso became firmly entrenched in the mindset of Australian coffee drinkers. This has inevitably fostered the growth of independent cafés, coffee houses and artisan roasters across cities, suburbs and coastal towns, to the extent that attempts by the corporate chains to establish a foothold on the Australian high street have, so far, famously failed.

You're unlikely to remember the exact time and place you tried your first great coffee. But no doubt you remember the ensuing frustration in trying to recapture that 'espresso moment'. Why doesn't every coffee have that perfect bittersweet balance and heady aroma? Luckily, today, good coffee is not so hard to find if you know where to look.

The 'flat white' is perhaps the most famous Antipodean style of coffee – I say Antipodean as it is hotly contested whether Australians or New Zealanders created the flat white. It is an espresso-based coffee with milk, made with a double shot in a 175-ml/6 fl oz.-cup and typically adorned with a latte art rosetta. It's been exported around the world by Australian and New Zealand expatriates who (like me) have opened cafés and coffee shops as a way of ensuring that they can get good coffee. Ironically, now even the big coffee chains have flat whites on their menus in an attempt to prove their coffee credentials. They're not fooling anyone.

BEETROOT REBOOT JUICE

Beetroot/beet, apples and kale are a killer combination for a natural energy drink, rich in iron and antioxidants.

2 medium beetroot/
    beets, washed and
    trimmed
2 red apples
a large handful of kale
    or spinach leaves

good squeeze of lemon
    juice to balance
    the sweetness
ice, to serve

SERVES 1

Feed the beetroot/beets, apples and kale or spinach leaves through the juicer and then add the lemon juice. Pour into a serving glass with ice.

SUNSHINE COAST JUICE

Far and away our most popular juice, this is a tribute to a beautiful stretch of coastline near my home town of Brisbane.

2 carrots, washed but
    unpeeled
1 Granny Smith apple
15 g/thumb-sized piece
    of fresh ginger,
    washed

100 ml/$\frac{1}{3}$ cup fresh
    orange juice (juice
    of approximately
    2 oranges)
ice, to serve

SERVES 1

Feed the carrots, apple and ginger through a vegetable juicer. Juice the orange with a regular juicer and then add it to the other juice and stir. Pour into a serving glass with ice.

AVOCADO, BANANA, HONEY & CHIA SMOOTHIE

Keep some peeled and halved bananas in sealed bags in the freezer ready to add to your smoothies. You can use unfrozen banana, but frozen ones give the smoothie a creamy texture.

$\frac{1}{2}$ avocado, pitted
$\frac{1}{2}$ frozen peeled banana
250 ml/1 cup oat, almond,
    cashew or soy milk

1 teaspoon clear honey
1 tablespoon chia seeds

SERVES 1

Scoop the flesh from the avocado into a blender. Add all the remaining ingredients and blitz until smooth. Pour into a glass and serve.

HIBISCUS ICED TEA

A refreshing and tart iced tea that can be made with tea bags if you can't find dried hibiscus flowers.

200 g/1 cup demerara/ turbinado sugar

HIBISCUS SYRUP
3 tablespoons edible dried hibiscus flowers
25 ml/1½ tablespoons sugar syrup

TO SERVE
ice cubes
mint sprigs
orange slices, halved

SERVES 4

To make the sugar syrup, put 200 ml/¾ cup of water into a saucepan, add the demerara/turbinado sugar and stir over a low heat until the sugar has dissolved. Remove from the heat, cool and store in the fridge for up to 1 month.

To make the hibiscus syrup, bring 1 litre/4 cups of water to the boil in a saucepan. Remove from the heat and allow to cool for 5 minutes. Add the hibiscus flowers and allow to steep for 1 hour. Strain into a large jug/pitcher and add the sugar syrup. Store in a sealed glass jar (unused syrup will keep in the fridge for a few days). Refrigerate for at least an hour before serving.

Serve in a tall glass with ice cubes, a sprig of mint and halved slices of orange.

GREEN GODDESS SMOOTHIE

Breakfast smoothies are a brilliant way of fuelling your body with lots of vitamins, fibre and antioxidants. This is one of my favourites with the ginger giving an energizing boost of flavour.

1 green pear, cored and chopped (leave the skin on)
40 g/2 cups fresh spinach
a thumb-sized piece of fresh ginger, peeled and chopped
½ teaspoon green matcha powder
250 ml/1 cup almond milk
1 heaped teaspoon almond butter
6 ice cubes

SERVES 1

Put all the ingredients into a blender and blitz until smooth. A high-speed blender will give the smoothest results. Pour into a glass and serve.

BEST EVER BLOODY MARY

- 500 ml/2 cups tomato juice
- 1 x Roast Tomatoes recipe (see page 57)
- 2 tablespoons Worcestershire sauce
- 2 tablespoons sriracha chilli/chili sauce
- a 3-cm/1¼-inch piece of fresh horseradish, peeled and finely grated
- 60 ml/¼ cup freshly squeezed lime juice
- 300 ml/1¼ cups vodka
- sea salt and freshly ground black pepper

TO GARNISH
Pickled Celery
(see below)
chilli/chile flakes

SERVES 4

Put the tomato juice and Roast Tomatoes in a food processor and blend until smooth.

Transfer to a jug/pitcher and stir in the Worcestershire sauce, sriracha chilli/chili sauce and grated horseradish. Season with salt and pepper, cover with clingfilm/plastic wrap and chill in the fridge for at least 30 minutes.

When ready to serve, add the lime juice and vodka, and stir well. Place a Pickled Celery stalk in four high-ball glasses, half-fill each glass with ice and pour in the Bloody Mary mixture. Garnish each with a pinch of chilli/chile flakes and enjoy!

PICKLED CELERY

- 1 head of celery, peeled and trimmed to stalks taller than your serving glasses
- 500 g/2½ cups caster/granulated sugar
- 1 litre/4 cups white wine vinegar
- 2 tablespoons sea salt
- 8 garlic cloves, chopped
- 2 teaspoons mustard seeds
- 2 teaspoons dried chilli/hot red pepper flakes
- 2 teaspoons black peppercorns

a tall sterilized glass jar with airtight lid

SERVES APPROX. 8

Stand the celery stalks in the tall, sterilized glass jar. Place all the remaining ingredients in a saucepan or pot with 250 ml/1 cup of water. Set over a medium-high heat and bring to the boil. Continue to boil for 15 minutes, then remove from the heat and cover to stop the liquor evaporating. Set aside to cool slightly, then pour into the jar containing the celery stalks. Wipe the jar clean and tightly screw on the lid. The celery is best made a day or two in advance. Store in the fridge for up to 1 month and once opened use within 1 week.

A Bloody Mary is the ultimate brunch drink, allowing you to ingest booze before midday with complete legitimacy and even a hint of old-fashioned sophistication. Roast Tomatoes add a deep and rich flavour and Pickled Celery gives a tangy zing, but you can substitute these for fresh tomatoes and raw celery if you're short of time.

HOMEMADE GINGERADE

Our homage to Queensland's Bundaberg Ginger Beer. I hope we've done you justice. For an alcoholic version of this recipe add 200 ml/¾ cup of vodka or gin.

200 g/1 cup demerara/
    turbinado sugar
40 g/4 tablespoons
    peeled and grated
    fresh ginger
freshly squeezed juice
    of 6–8 limes

a bunch of mint leaves,
    gently bruised
ice cubes
soda water, to top up
lime slices, to serve

SERVES 6

Place the sugar, grated ginger and 250 ml/ 1 cup of water in a saucepan or pot set over a medium heat. Stir continuously until the sugar has dissolved. Bring to the boil, then immediately reduce the heat and simmer gently for 10 minutes. Remove the pan from the heat and set aside to cool for at least 1 hour. The longer it infuses the more gingery your syrup.

Add the lime juice and bruised mint leaves.

Half-fill your serving jug or highball glasses with ice. Pour in the ginger-lime syrup (about 60 ml/¼ cup per person). Top up with soda water, add lime slices, and serve.

PINK FIZZ

If you ever needed encouragement to drink at breakfast time, this will do it.

200 g/1 cup caster/
    granulated sugar
1 tablespoon edible
    dried hibiscus flowers
Prosecco or champagne,
    to top up

SERVES 6

Place the sugar, 500 ml/2 cups of water and the hibiscus flowers in a saucepan or pot set over a medium heat. Stir continuously until the sugar has dissolved. Bring to the boil, then remove the pan from the heat and allow the mixture to infuse for 20 minutes. Strain the syrup through a fine mesh sieve/strainer set over a large mixing bowl, then set aside to cool.

Pour into an airtight bottle or container and chill in the fridge until ready to use. Store any unused syrup in the fridge for up to 1 month.

Pour 15 ml/1 tablespoon of the hibiscus syrup into the base of each champagne flute. Top up with Prosecco or champagne and serve.

INDEX

ACKNOWLEDGMENTS

A world of thanks to:

The team at Ryland Peters & Small for reassuring me that the world needs another cookbook and taking a punt on me, twice.

Our lovely customers, some of whom have been coming through our doors for 10 years, this book is for you.

The entire Lantana team but especially the chefs, past and present, who have been instrumental in the success of the cafés.

Michael Homan, co founder of Lantana and my brother-in-law, for allowing me to focus on the fun stuff while you sharpen the pencils and keep the business running. Ten years in and we are still friends. Who says family members can't work together?

My sister Caitlin, our other co-founder, you are untiring in your positivity and support and you were instrumental in convincing us to open an Australian café in London.

Mat, I always knew you had impeccable taste but in the process of writing this book I've discovered that you have many hidden talents; proofreader, food critic, recipe tester and cheerleader.

Vinnie and Esther, always welcome distractions.

My mum, who dutifully cooked for us for many years to a scheduled meal plan. I'm glad that the tables have turned and you now get to enjoy meals cooked by your four appreciative children.

Lastly, my dad, who nurtured my love of eating and cooking and taught me the art of being a good host. I wish you had been able to see Lantana. I think you would approve.